I0711397

Get A Free Book At: xspurts.com/posts/free-book-offer

Table of Contents:

Understanding Judgment

Judgment is an inherent aspect of human cognition and behavior, often influencing how individuals perceive, interact with, and make decisions about the world around them. From social interactions to professional environments, the psychology of being judgmental plays a significant role in shaping our thoughts, attitudes, and behaviors.

At its core, judgment involves the process of forming opinions or evaluations about people, situations, or events based on available information and personal beliefs. It encompasses a wide range of cognitive processes, including perception, interpretation, and evaluation. However, while judgment can be a useful tool for navigating complex social environments and making decisions, it can also have negative consequences when it becomes overly critical or biased.

One of the key factors influencing judgment is perception. Individuals often rely on their perceptions of others to form opinions and make decisions. However, perceptions can be subjective and influenced by various factors such as past experiences, cultural norms, and personal biases. For example, someone who has had negative experiences with a certain group of people may be more likely to judge individuals from that group harshly, regardless of their actual behavior.

Another important aspect of judgment is interpretation. When faced with ambiguous or incomplete information, individuals often rely on their interpretations to fill in the gaps and make sense of the situation. However, these interpretations can be influenced by pre-existing beliefs and stereotypes, leading to biased judgments. For instance, someone who holds stereotypes about certain professions may automatically assume that individuals in those professions possess certain traits or characteristics, regardless of whether this is true or not.

Evaluation is the final stage of the judgment process, where individuals make decisions or form opinions based on their perceptions and interpretations. These evaluations can range from simple judgments about someone's appearance to more complex assessments of their character or abilities. However, evaluations can also be influenced by factors such as emotions, social norms, and personal values. For example, someone who values honesty may judge others more positively if they perceive them as being honest, while someone who values ambition may judge others more harshly if they perceive them as being lazy or unmotivated.

While judgment is a natural and often necessary aspect of human cognition, it is essential to recognize its potential pitfalls and biases. Being overly judgmental can lead to misunderstandings, conflict, and discrimination, both in personal and professional settings. Therefore, it is important to approach judgment with awareness, empathy, and an openness to challenging our own assumptions and biases.

In conclusion, the psychology of being judgmental is a complex and multifaceted phenomenon that influences how individuals perceive, interpret, and evaluate the world around them. While judgment can be a useful tool for navigating social interactions and making decisions, it can also lead to biases, misunderstandings, and discrimination if not approached with awareness and empathy. By understanding the various factors that influence judgment and cultivating a mindset of openness and critical thinking, we can strive to make more informed and fair judgments in our daily lives.

Conceptualizing Judgment

Judgment is a fundamental aspect of human cognition, encompassing the process of forming opinions, making evaluations, and drawing conclusions about the world around us. It plays a crucial role in our daily interactions, influencing how we perceive others, make decisions, and navigate social situations. However, the psychology of being judgmental involves a complex interplay of cognitive processes, emotions, and social factors.

At its core, judgment involves the interpretation and evaluation of information based on personal beliefs, experiences, and values. It begins with the perception of stimuli from the environment, including verbal and non-verbal cues, which are then processed and interpreted by the brain. These interpretations are influenced by a variety of factors, such as past experiences, cultural norms, and individual differences.

Once information has been interpreted, individuals engage in the process of evaluation, where they assign meaning and significance to the stimuli. This involves comparing the perceived information to existing schemas or mental frameworks, which help categorize and make sense of the world. However, evaluations can also be influenced by biases, stereotypes, and heuristics, leading to inaccurate or unfair judgments.

One common bias that affects judgment is the confirmation bias, where individuals tend to seek out information that confirms their pre-existing beliefs or hypotheses while ignoring contradictory evidence. This can lead to a reinforcement of existing stereotypes and prejudices, perpetuating unfair or discriminatory judgments. Similarly, the availability heuristic can cause individuals to rely on easily accessible information when making judgments, rather than considering the full range of evidence.

Emotions also play a significant role in the judgment process, influencing how information is perceived, interpreted, and evaluated. For example, individuals may be more likely to make harsher judgments when they are feeling angry or threatened, while positive emotions may lead to more lenient evaluations. Additionally, social factors such as group dynamics and social norms can shape judgment, as individuals may conform to the opinions of others or adjust their judgments to fit in with the group.

The psychology of being judgmental also involves understanding the consequences of judgment, both for individuals and society as a whole. Harsh or unfair judgments can have a detrimental impact on individuals' self-esteem, relationships, and mental health, leading to feelings of alienation, rejection, and inadequacy. Furthermore, discriminatory judgments based on factors such as race, gender, or sexual orientation can perpetuate inequality and social injustice.

However, judgment is not inherently negative, and it serves an essential function in human cognition and behavior. When approached with awareness and mindfulness, judgment can help individuals make informed decisions, navigate social interactions, and protect themselves from harm. By cultivating empathy, critical thinking, and an openness to new perspectives, individuals can strive to make more fair, compassionate, and constructive judgments in their daily lives.

History and Evolution of Judgment

The history and evolution of judgment are deeply intertwined with the development of human cognition and social behavior. Since ancient times, humans have relied on judgment to make sense of the world around them, formulating opinions, and making decisions based on their observations and experiences. The concept of judgment has evolved over the centuries, shaped by philosophical, psychological, and sociocultural influences.

In ancient Greek philosophy, scholars such as Socrates, Plato, and Aristotle explored the nature of judgment and its role in human reasoning. Socrates famously asserted that "the unexamined life is not worth living," emphasizing the importance of critical self-reflection and inquiry in the process of judgment. Plato's allegory of the cave highlighted the role of perception and interpretation in shaping individuals' understanding of reality, while Aristotle's theory of virtue ethics emphasized the importance of practical wisdom in making moral judgments.

During the Enlightenment period, thinkers such as René Descartes, John Locke, and Immanuel Kant furthered the study of judgment, laying the groundwork for modern psychology and philosophy. Descartes' dualism posited a distinction between the mind and body, leading to a focus on rationality and introspection in the process of judgment. Locke's empiricism emphasized the role of sensory experience and observation in forming beliefs and opinions, while Kant's transcendental idealism explored the universal principles that govern human judgment.

In the early 20th century, psychologists such as Sigmund Freud and Carl Jung expanded the study of judgment to include unconscious processes and motivations. Freud's psychoanalytic theory introduced the concept of defense mechanisms, such as projection and displacement, which influence individuals' perceptions and judgments of themselves and others. Jung's theories of archetypes and the collective unconscious explored the deeper layers of human consciousness that shape our judgments and behaviors.

Throughout the 20th century, advancements in cognitive psychology and social psychology furthered our understanding of judgment and decision-making processes. Researchers such as Daniel Kahneman and Amos Tversky revolutionized the field with their work on heuristics and biases, revealing the systematic errors that humans make when judging probabilities and making decisions under uncertainty. The study of social judgment, pioneered by scholars like Muzafer Sherif and Solomon Asch, highlighted the role of social influence and conformity in shaping individuals' judgments and attitudes.

In contemporary psychology, the study of judgment continues to be a vibrant area of research, encompassing topics such as moral judgment, intuitive judgment, and the neuroscience of decision-making. Cognitive scientists use advanced imaging techniques such as functional magnetic resonance imaging (fMRI) to study the neural mechanisms underlying judgment and decision-making processes. Social psychologists explore the factors that influence group dynamics, intergroup relations, and the formation of stereotypes and prejudices.

In conclusion, the history and evolution of judgment reflect humanity's ongoing quest to understand the complexities of human cognition and behavior. From ancient philosophy to modern psychology, scholars have sought to unravel the mysteries of judgment and decision-making, shedding light on the cognitive, emotional, and social processes that shape our perceptions of the world. By understanding the history of judgment, we can gain insight into the fundamental aspects of human nature and strive to make more informed, compassionate, and rational judgments in our daily lives.

Unmasking Judgemental Behavior

Judgmental behavior is a complex phenomenon deeply rooted in human psychology and social interaction. It involves forming critical opinions or evaluations about others based on perceived characteristics, behaviors, or beliefs. While judgment can serve important cognitive functions, such as making sense of the world and ensuring personal safety, it can also lead to biases, stereotypes, and interpersonal conflicts when taken to extremes.

One of the key aspects of judgmental behavior is the tendency to categorize people into simplified groups or stereotypes based on superficial characteristics such as appearance, ethnicity, gender, or socioeconomic status. This categorization process, known as social categorization, is a natural cognitive shortcut that allows individuals to quickly process vast amounts of information and make decisions efficiently. However, it can also lead to oversimplified and inaccurate perceptions of others, contributing to prejudice and discrimination.

Another factor that influences judgmental behavior is the human tendency to rely on heuristics or mental shortcuts when making judgments and decisions. These heuristics, while often useful in everyday life, can also lead to cognitive biases that distort our perceptions and judgments of others. For example, the halo effect is a cognitive bias in which a person's positive qualities or attributes overshadow any negative qualities they may possess. This can lead to biased judgments based on superficial factors such as physical attractiveness or charisma.

Social psychologists have identified several factors that contribute to judgmental behavior, including social norms, cultural values, and individual differences in personality traits. For example, individuals who score high on measures of authoritarianism or social dominance orientation are more likely to exhibit judgmental behavior, as they tend to view the world in terms of hierarchical power dynamics and social dominance.

Moreover, situational factors such as stress, fatigue, or time pressure can also influence judgmental behavior by impairing cognitive functioning and increasing reliance on automatic, heuristic-based thinking. In such situations, individuals may be more likely to rely on stereotypes or prejudices to make quick judgments without carefully considering all available information.

It is important to recognize that judgmental behavior is not necessarily indicative of malicious intent or character flaws. In many cases, it is a product of cognitive biases and social conditioning that operate at a subconscious level. However, unchecked judgmental behavior can have negative consequences for both individuals and society as a whole, leading to discrimination, social exclusion, and interpersonal conflict.

One way to mitigate judgmental behavior is through increased self-awareness and mindfulness. By recognizing our own biases and cognitive shortcuts, we can learn to challenge them and adopt a more nuanced and empathetic approach to understanding others. Additionally, fostering empathy and open-mindedness can help us overcome stereotypes and prejudices and form more accurate and compassionate judgments of others.

In conclusion, judgmental behavior is a complex and multifaceted phenomenon influenced by cognitive, social, and situational factors. While it serves important cognitive functions, such as making sense of the world and ensuring personal safety, it can also lead to biases, stereotypes, and interpersonal conflicts when taken to extremes. By increasing self-awareness, fostering empathy, and challenging our own biases, we can work towards overcoming judgmental behavior and promoting a more inclusive and compassionate society.

Types of Judgment

Judgment is a fundamental aspect of human cognition and plays a significant role in how we navigate social interactions and make decisions. It involves forming opinions, evaluations, or assessments about people, situations, or events based on available information. There are various types of judgment that individuals employ in different contexts, each with its own cognitive processes and implications.

One common type of judgment is social judgment, which involves forming opinions about other people based on their behavior, appearance, or social status. Social judgments can range from simple impressions or evaluations to more complex assessments of personality traits, motives, or intentions. These judgments often rely on heuristic cues such as facial expressions, body language, or verbal cues to make rapid assessments of others.

Another type of judgment is moral judgment, which involves evaluating the rightness or wrongness of actions, behaviors, or decisions based on moral principles or ethical standards. Moral judgments are influenced by cultural norms, personal values, and social context, and can vary widely across individuals and cultures. They play a crucial role in guiding behavior and moral decision-making, shaping attitudes towards issues such as fairness, justice, and responsibility.

Judgments can also be cognitive in nature, involving assessments of probability, likelihood, or causality. These judgments are based on logical reasoning, empirical evidence, or statistical analysis and play a crucial role in problem-solving, decision-making, and critical thinking. Cognitive judgments can range from simple assessments of probability, such as estimating the likelihood of an event occurring, to more complex evaluations of causality or logical validity.

In addition to social and moral judgments, individuals also engage in self-judgment, which involves evaluating their own thoughts, feelings, and behaviors. Self-judgments can be positive or negative and can have significant implications for self-esteem, self-concept, and psychological well-being. They are influenced by factors such as social comparison, feedback from others, and internalized standards or expectations.

Furthermore, individuals often make aesthetic judgments, which involve assessing the beauty, attractiveness, or aesthetic appeal of people, objects, or environments. Aesthetic judgments are subjective and influenced by individual preferences, cultural norms, and personal experiences. They play a role in shaping preferences, tastes, and aesthetic experiences, and can have implications for social interactions, consumer behavior, and artistic expression.

Finally, individuals also make legal judgments, which involve interpreting and applying laws, rules, or regulations to specific cases or situations. Legal judgments are guided by legal principles, precedents, and statutes and play a crucial role in the administration of justice, dispute resolution, and the protection of individual rights and freedoms.

In conclusion, judgment is a multifaceted cognitive process that involves forming opinions, evaluations, or assessments about people, situations, or events based on available information. There are various types of judgment, including social, moral, cognitive, self, aesthetic, and legal judgments, each with its own cognitive processes and implications. Understanding these different types of judgment can help individuals navigate social interactions, make informed decisions, and cultivate empathy and understanding towards others.

Psychological Perspectives of Judgment

Psychological perspectives offer valuable insights into the complexities of judgment, shedding light on the cognitive processes, underlying mechanisms, and socio-cultural influences that shape our propensity to be judgmental. Several psychological theories and frameworks provide a deeper understanding of why individuals engage in judgmental behavior and how it impacts interpersonal relationships, decision-making, and overall well-being.

One such perspective is social cognition theory, which posits that individuals are inherently motivated to understand and interpret the social world around them. According to this theory, people rely on cognitive shortcuts or heuristics to make rapid judgments about others, often based on limited information or stereotypes. These automatic processes can lead to biased judgments and perceptions, as individuals may rely on preconceived notions or societal norms rather than objective evidence.

Attribution theory is another psychological framework that explores how individuals attribute causes to behavior, events, or outcomes. When making judgments about others, people tend to attribute behavior to either internal factors (e.g., personality traits) or external factors (e.g., situational factors). Attribution biases, such as the fundamental attribution error or actor-observer bias, can influence how individuals perceive and interpret others' behavior, leading to inaccurate or unfair judgments.

Social identity theory emphasizes the role of social categorization and ingroup-outgroup dynamics in shaping judgmental behavior. Individuals tend to categorize others based on shared characteristics or group memberships, such as race, gender, or nationality. Ingroup favoritism and outgroup derogation can lead to biased judgments and discriminatory attitudes towards those perceived as different or belonging to a different social group.

Additionally, cognitive dissonance theory suggests that individuals experience discomfort when their beliefs or attitudes conflict with their behavior or experiences. To reduce this cognitive dissonance, people may engage in rationalization or justification processes, which can involve making biased judgments or evaluations of others to maintain consistency with their existing beliefs or self-concept.

From a socio-cultural perspective, judgmental behavior can be influenced by societal norms, cultural values, and socialization processes. Cultural differences in collectivism versus individualism, power distance, and uncertainty avoidance can shape how people perceive and evaluate others' behavior. Cultural stereotypes and societal expectations may also contribute to the formation of biased judgments based on factors such as race, gender, or socioeconomic status.

Furthermore, evolutionary psychology offers insights into the adaptive functions of judgmental behavior in human evolution. From an evolutionary perspective, making quick assessments of others' trustworthiness, competence, or intentions may have conferred survival advantages in ancestral environments. However, these evolutionary predispositions can also lead to cognitive biases and errors in modern-day contexts, where the social landscape is more complex and diverse.

In conclusion, psychological perspectives provide a multifaceted understanding of judgmental behavior, highlighting the cognitive, social, and cultural factors that influence how individuals form opinions, evaluations, or assessments of others. By examining the underlying processes and biases involved in judgment, psychologists can offer strategies for promoting empathy, reducing prejudice, and fostering more constructive and open-minded interactions in society.

Cognitive Mechanisms of Judgments

Cognitive mechanisms play a fundamental role in the formation and expression of judgments, influencing how individuals perceive, interpret, and evaluate information about themselves and others. Understanding these cognitive processes is essential for comprehending the psychology of being judgmental.

One crucial cognitive mechanism involved in judgment is schema activation. Schemas are mental frameworks or templates that help individuals organize and interpret incoming information. When encountering a new situation or individual, people often rely on existing schemas to make sense of the world around them. However, schemas can also lead to biased judgments when individuals apply them rigidly or without considering additional information. For example, stereotypes are a type of schema that can influence how people judge others based on characteristics such as race, gender, or occupation.

Another cognitive mechanism relevant to judgment is the availability heuristic. This heuristic involves individuals' tendency to rely on information that is readily available in their memory when making judgments or decisions. For instance, if someone recalls recent negative experiences with a particular group of people, they may be more likely to form negative judgments about individuals belonging to that group. The availability heuristic can lead to biased judgments when individuals overestimate the prevalence or significance of certain information based on its accessibility in memory.

Anchoring and adjustment is another cognitive process that influences judgment. This mechanism describes individuals' tendency to rely heavily on initial pieces of information (anchors) when making subsequent judgments or evaluations, even if those initial pieces of information are irrelevant or inaccurate. Once individuals anchor on a particular value or attribute, they may adjust their judgment only slightly, leading to biased or incomplete evaluations. For example, if someone receives negative feedback about a colleague, they may anchor on that information and overlook the colleague's positive qualities when forming judgments about their competence or character.

Confirmation bias is a cognitive bias that influences how individuals seek, interpret, and remember information in a way that confirms their existing beliefs or expectations. When people hold preconceived notions or judgments about others, they are more likely to selectively attend to information that supports those judgments while ignoring or discounting contradictory evidence. Confirmation bias can perpetuate and reinforce judgmental attitudes, as individuals seek out information that validates their existing opinions while dismissing evidence that challenges them.

Attributional processes also play a significant role in judgment, particularly in how individuals attribute causes to behavior or outcomes. When evaluating others' behavior, people may make attributions based on internal factors (e.g., personality traits) or external factors (e.g., situational circumstances). However, individuals' attributions can be biased by factors such as self-serving biases, in-group biases, or the fundamental attribution error, leading to inaccurate or unfair judgments about others.

In summary, cognitive mechanisms such as schema activation, the availability heuristic, anchoring and adjustment, confirmation bias, and attributional processes shape how individuals form judgments about themselves and others. By understanding these cognitive processes, psychologists can develop interventions aimed at reducing judgmental attitudes and promoting more accurate, fair, and empathetic interactions in society.

Cognitive Biases in Judgment

Cognitive biases are inherent shortcuts in our thinking processes that can lead to systematic errors in judgment and decision-making. They stem from the brain's attempts to simplify complex information processing tasks, but they can also result in skewed perceptions and inaccurate assessments. Understanding these cognitive biases is essential in comprehending the psychology of being judgmental.

One common cognitive bias is the confirmation bias, which involves the tendency to search for, interpret, and remember information that confirms one's preexisting beliefs or hypotheses while disregarding contradictory evidence. When individuals are judgmental, they may selectively attend to information that aligns with their existing judgments about others, reinforcing their biases and leading to inaccurate assessments.

Another cognitive bias relevant to judgment is the availability heuristic, which describes the tendency to overestimate the likelihood or importance of events based on their ease of recall from memory. For instance, if someone has had a negative experience with a particular group of people, they may perceive that group as more prevalent or influential than it actually is, leading to biased judgments about its members.

Anchoring bias is another cognitive bias that influences judgment. It occurs when individuals rely too heavily on initial pieces of information (anchors) when making subsequent judgments or decisions, even if those initial pieces of information are irrelevant or inaccurate. For example, if someone hears negative gossip about a coworker, they may anchor on that information and overlook the coworker's positive qualities when forming judgments about them.

The fundamental attribution error is a cognitive bias that involves attributing others' behavior to internal characteristics (e.g., personality traits) while underestimating the influence of situational factors. When individuals are judgmental, they may attribute others' behavior to dispositional factors rather than considering external circumstances, leading to unfair or inaccurate judgments.

The halo effect is a cognitive bias in which one's overall impression of a person influences their perceptions of that person's specific traits or abilities. For example, if someone finds a person physically attractive, they may assume that person possesses other positive qualities, such as intelligence or kindness, even without evidence to support those assumptions. This bias can lead to biased judgments based on superficial characteristics rather than objective criteria.

In-group bias is another cognitive bias that influences judgment. It involves favoring members of one's own group over members of out-groups, leading to unfair treatment or evaluations of those outside one's group. When individuals are judgmental, they may show preference or leniency towards members of their in-group while being more critical or hostile towards members of out-groups.

The mere exposure effect is a cognitive bias that describes the tendency to develop a preference for things or people simply because they are familiar. When individuals repeatedly encounter certain individuals or groups, they may develop more positive attitudes towards them, regardless of their actual characteristics or qualities. This bias can contribute to judgmental attitudes based on familiarity rather than objective assessment.

In conclusion, cognitive biases such as confirmation bias, availability heuristic, anchoring bias, fundamental attribution error, halo effect, in-group bias, and mere exposure effect play significant roles in shaping judgmental attitudes and behaviors. By understanding these biases, individuals can become more aware of their own judgmental tendencies and work towards making more accurate and unbiased assessments of others.

Influence of Perception in Judgment

Perception plays a crucial role in shaping our judgments and interpretations of the world around us. It influences how we perceive and evaluate others, situations, and events, ultimately impacting our behavior and decision-making processes. Understanding the influence of perception on judgment is essential in comprehending the psychology of being judgmental.

One significant aspect of perception that influences judgment is selective attention. Selective attention refers to the tendency to focus on certain aspects of our environment while ignoring others. When individuals are judgmental, they may selectively attend to information that confirms their existing beliefs or biases about others, leading to skewed perceptions and inaccurate judgments. For example, if someone has a negative opinion of a particular group of people, they may only notice instances that reinforce their negative beliefs while disregarding evidence to the contrary.

Another aspect of perception that affects judgment is interpretation. Interpretation involves assigning meaning to sensory information based on our past experiences, beliefs, and expectations. When individuals are judgmental, they may interpret ambiguous or ambiguous information in a way that aligns with their preconceived notions or stereotypes about others. For instance, if someone has a negative perception of a coworker, they may interpret the coworker's actions in a negative light, even if those actions could be interpreted differently by someone with a more neutral perspective.

Stereotypes also influence perception and judgment. Stereotypes are generalized beliefs or assumptions about a particular group of people based on characteristics such as race, gender, or age. When individuals are judgmental, they may rely on stereotypes to form judgments about others without considering individual differences or nuances. For example, if someone holds stereotypes about older adults being technologically inept, they may assume that an older coworker is incapable of learning new software, even if the coworker is actually proficient in technology.

Perceptual set is another factor that influences judgment. Perceptual set refers to the tendency to perceive and interpret information in a particular way based on our past experiences, expectations, and motivations. When individuals are judgmental, their perceptual set may predispose them to perceive others in a certain light, regardless of the actual circumstances. For example, if someone has had negative experiences with authority figures in the past, they may perceive their boss as controlling or unfair, even if their boss's behavior is objectively reasonable.

Emotional state also plays a role in perception and judgment. Our emotional state can color our perceptions of others and influence the judgments we make about them. When individuals are judgmental, negative emotions such as anger, fear, or jealousy can distort their perceptions and lead to harsh or unfair judgments. For example, if someone is feeling insecure about their own abilities, they may perceive a colleague's success as a threat and judge them harshly as a result.

In conclusion, perception significantly influences judgment, shaping how we perceive and evaluate others. Factors such as selective attention, interpretation, stereotypes, perceptual set, and emotional state all play roles in determining our perceptions and judgments of others. By understanding the influence of perception on judgment, individuals can become more aware of their own biases and work towards making more accurate and fair assessments of others.

Social Constructs and Judgement

Social constructs are the frameworks through which society perceives and understands various aspects of life, including behaviors, identities, and norms. These constructs significantly influence how individuals form judgments about others and the world around them, contributing to the psychology of being judgmental.

One prominent social construct that shapes judgment is cultural norms and values. Every culture has its own set of norms, beliefs, and values that dictate what is considered acceptable or unacceptable behavior. Individuals often judge others based on how well they adhere to these cultural norms. For example, in some cultures, punctuality is highly valued, and individuals who are consistently late may be judged as irresponsible or disrespectful.

Gender roles and expectations are another social construct that influences judgment. Society often imposes rigid expectations about how individuals should behave based on their gender. Men and women who deviate from these gender norms may be subject to judgment and criticism. For instance, a woman who displays assertive behavior may be labeled as aggressive, while a man who shows vulnerability may be seen as weak.

Social status and socioeconomic status also play a significant role in judgment. Individuals from lower socioeconomic backgrounds may be judged negatively by those in higher social classes, leading to stereotypes and biases. Similarly, individuals with higher social status may be judged more favorably, regardless of their actual behavior or character.

Race and ethnicity are powerful social constructs that shape judgment and perception. Racial stereotypes and biases can lead to unfair and discriminatory judgments about individuals based solely on their race or ethnicity. For example, individuals from minority racial or ethnic groups may be subjected to stereotypes that portray them as lazy, dangerous, or unintelligent.

Another social construct that influences judgment is physical appearance. Society often places a high value on physical attractiveness, and individuals who do not meet societal standards of beauty may be judged harshly. This can lead to discrimination and bias against individuals who are overweight, have physical disabilities, or do not conform to traditional standards of beauty.

Education and intellectualism are also social constructs that shape judgment. Individuals with higher levels of education or intelligence may be perceived as more competent, trustworthy, and worthy of respect. Conversely, those with lower levels of education or intellectual ability may be judged as inferior or less capable.

Religion and spirituality are important social constructs that influence judgment and perception. Individuals who adhere to certain religious beliefs may judge others based on whether they conform to those beliefs or not. This can lead to discrimination and prejudice against individuals who belong to different religious or spiritual traditions.

In conclusion, social constructs significantly influence how individuals form judgments about others. Cultural norms, gender roles, social status, race and ethnicity, physical appearance, education, religion, and spirituality all play roles in shaping judgment and perception. By recognizing the influence of these social constructs, individuals can work towards overcoming biases and making more fair and equitable judgments about others.

The Role of Society in Judgment Formation

Society plays a significant role in shaping the way individuals form judgments about others and the world around them. From cultural norms to media portrayals, societal influences heavily impact the psychology of being judgmental.

Cultural norms and values are central to society's role in judgment formation. Each culture has its own set of beliefs, customs, and traditions that dictate what is considered acceptable or unacceptable behavior. Individuals internalize these cultural norms from a young age and use them as a framework for judging others. For example, cultures that prioritize collectivism may view individualistic behaviors as selfish or inappropriate, leading to judgments against individuals who prioritize their own needs over the needs of the group.

Media also plays a crucial role in shaping judgment formation. Television shows, movies, advertisements, and social media platforms often perpetuate stereotypes and biases that influence how individuals perceive different groups of people. For instance, media representations of certain racial or ethnic groups as criminals or terrorists can lead to negative judgments and discrimination against individuals belonging to those groups in real life.

Peer pressure and social influence are powerful forces that shape judgment within society. People often conform to the opinions and behaviors of their peers in order to fit in and avoid social rejection. This can lead individuals to adopt the same judgments and biases as their social circle, even if they personally disagree with them. For example, a person may judge someone negatively simply because their friends or colleagues express similar opinions.

Institutional factors, such as laws, policies, and organizational culture, also influence judgment formation within society. Institutions can perpetuate systemic biases and discrimination through their practices and procedures. For example, discriminatory hiring practices or unequal access to resources based on factors such as race, gender, or socioeconomic status can reinforce negative stereotypes and lead to biased judgments against certain groups of people.

Socialization processes, including education and family upbringing, contribute to the development of judgmental attitudes and behaviors. Children learn from their parents, teachers, and other authority figures about what is considered right and wrong, acceptable and unacceptable. These early lessons shape their understanding of the world and influence how they judge others. For instance, children who are raised in environments that emphasize tolerance and empathy are more likely to form non-judgmental attitudes towards others.

Religious and moral beliefs also play a role in judgment formation within society. Many religions and moral philosophies teach their followers to adhere to certain ethical principles and to judge others based on those principles. However, interpretations of religious teachings and moral codes can vary widely, leading to differences in judgment among individuals and groups.

In conclusion, society plays a multifaceted role in shaping the way individuals form judgments about others. Cultural norms, media portrayals, peer pressure, institutional factors, socialization processes, and religious and moral beliefs all contribute to the psychology of being judgmental. By understanding these societal influences, individuals can work towards overcoming biases and fostering a more inclusive and empathetic society.

Societal Conditioning and Stereotypes

Societal conditioning and stereotypes are intricately connected to the psychology of being judgmental, influencing how individuals perceive and interact with others. Throughout history, societies have developed norms, values, and stereotypes that shape people's attitudes and behaviors towards different social groups.

Societal conditioning refers to the process by which individuals internalize the values, beliefs, and norms of their society through socialization. From a young age, people are exposed to various social influences, including family, education, media, and peer groups, which contribute to the formation of their worldview and attitudes towards others. These societal influences often perpetuate stereotypes, which are oversimplified and generalized beliefs about a particular group of people.

Stereotypes are mental shortcuts that people use to categorize individuals based on their membership in a particular social group, such as race, gender, ethnicity, or socioeconomic status. While stereotypes can sometimes be based on partial truths or observations, they often oversimplify complex realities and lead to biased judgments and discriminatory behaviors.

For example, racial stereotypes, such as the belief that certain ethnic groups are more prone to criminal behavior, can lead to racial profiling and discrimination in law enforcement and criminal justice systems. Similarly, gender stereotypes, such as the belief that women are inherently less competent than men in leadership roles, can contribute to gender-based discrimination in the workplace.

Societal conditioning and stereotypes are perpetuated and reinforced through various social institutions and media channels. For instance, mass media often portrays certain groups in stereotypical ways, which can influence public perceptions and reinforce existing biases. Additionally, educational curricula may contain biased or incomplete representations of history and culture, contributing to the perpetuation of stereotypes and prejudices.

The influence of societal conditioning and stereotypes extends beyond individual attitudes and behaviors to impact systemic inequalities and social structures. For example, institutional racism and sexism are deeply entrenched in many societies, resulting in disparities in access to opportunities and resources based on race and gender. These systemic inequalities perpetuate stereotypes and contribute to the marginalization and oppression of certain groups.

Overcoming societal conditioning and stereotypes requires individuals to engage in critical self-reflection and actively challenge their own beliefs and assumptions. It also requires collective efforts to address systemic inequalities and promote diversity, equity, and inclusion in all areas of society.

Education and awareness-raising campaigns can play a crucial role in challenging stereotypes and promoting empathy and understanding among different social groups. By providing accurate and diverse representations of people from various backgrounds, education can help counteract the negative effects of stereotypes and foster more inclusive attitudes and behaviors.

Additionally, efforts to increase diversity and representation in media, politics, and other influential spheres can help challenge stereotypes and promote positive social change. By amplifying the voices and experiences of marginalized groups, society can work towards dismantling systemic inequalities and creating a more just and equitable world for all.

In conclusion, societal conditioning and stereotypes are deeply ingrained in the psychology of being judgmental, shaping people's attitudes and behaviors towards others. Overcoming these biases requires individual and collective efforts to challenge stereotypes, promote empathy and understanding, and address systemic inequalities in society. By working together to challenge stereotypes and promote diversity and inclusion, we can create a more equitable and compassionate world for future generations.

Judgments and Emotions

Judgments and emotions are closely intertwined in the psychology of being judgmental, influencing how individuals perceive and react to the world around them. While judgments are often based on rational thought and analysis, emotions play a significant role in shaping and reinforcing these judgments.

Emotions are complex psychological states that involve subjective feelings, physiological responses, and behavioral reactions. They can range from positive emotions like happiness and excitement to negative emotions like anger and sadness. Emotions can influence cognitive processes such as attention, memory, and decision-making, making them essential factors in the formation of judgments.

When individuals make judgments about others, their emotions can color their perceptions and evaluations. For example, if someone is feeling angry or resentful towards a particular person or group, they may be more likely to make negative judgments about them, even if those judgments are not based on objective evidence. Similarly, positive emotions like affection or admiration can lead to more favorable judgments about others.

Emotions can also influence the way individuals interpret and respond to information. Research has shown that people are more likely to perceive ambiguous or neutral stimuli in a way that aligns with their emotional state. For example, someone who is feeling anxious or fearful may interpret a neutral facial expression as hostile or threatening.

In addition to influencing the formation of judgments, emotions also play a crucial role in how judgments are expressed and communicated. For example, when individuals express their judgments, they may convey their emotions through nonverbal cues such as facial expressions, body language, and tone of voice. These emotional cues can affect how judgments are received and interpreted by others.

Moreover, emotions can also influence the way judgments are remembered and recalled over time. Research has shown that emotional events are more likely to be remembered than neutral events, a phenomenon known as the emotional enhancement of memory. Therefore, individuals may be more likely to remember and recall judgments that were made in highly emotional states, leading to the reinforcement of those judgments over time.

The relationship between judgments and emotions is bidirectional, meaning that judgments can also influence emotions. For example, when individuals make judgments about others, they may experience emotions such as guilt, shame, or pride, depending on the nature of their judgments. These emotions can then influence subsequent judgments and behaviors.

In some cases, the interplay between judgments and emotions can lead to cognitive biases and irrational thinking. For example, confirmation bias is the tendency to seek out information that confirms preexisting beliefs or judgments while ignoring contradictory evidence. Emotional biases, such as the halo effect, can also lead individuals to make judgments based on irrelevant emotional associations rather than objective criteria.

To mitigate the negative effects of judgments and emotions, individuals can practice mindfulness and self-awareness to recognize and regulate their emotional responses. Additionally, fostering empathy and perspective-taking can help individuals understand the perspectives and experiences of others, leading to more compassionate and empathetic judgments.

In conclusion, judgments and emotions are deeply intertwined in the psychology of being judgmental, influencing how individuals perceive, evaluate, and respond to the world around them. By understanding the complex interplay between judgments and emotions, individuals can develop greater self-awareness, empathy, and rationality in their decision-making processes.

Interplay of Emotions in Judgment Formation

The interplay of emotions in judgment formation is a fascinating aspect of human psychology that sheds light on how individuals perceive and evaluate the world around them. Emotions play a significant role in shaping judgments, influencing both the cognitive processes involved in decision-making and the subjective interpretation of information.

Emotions are complex psychological states that involve subjective feelings, physiological responses, and behavioral reactions. They can range from basic emotions like happiness, sadness, anger, fear, and disgust to more complex emotions like pride, jealousy, and guilt. These emotions can arise in response to internal or external stimuli and can have a profound impact on cognitive processes, memory, attention, and behavior.

In the context of judgment formation, emotions can influence how individuals perceive and interpret information. For example, research has shown that individuals in positive emotional states are more likely to make optimistic judgments about uncertain situations, while those in negative emotional states may be more pessimistic or risk-averse. This phenomenon, known as affective forecasting, highlights how emotions can bias individuals' predictions about future outcomes.

Moreover, emotions can also shape the salience of information and the way it is processed. For instance, individuals tend to pay more attention to emotionally charged stimuli and may prioritize processing information that elicits strong emotional responses. This selective attention to emotional cues can influence the judgments individuals make based on the information available to them.

Emotions can also influence the evaluation and interpretation of social cues, such as facial expressions, body language, and vocal tone. For example, individuals may perceive ambiguous social signals in a way that aligns with their emotional state, leading to biased judgments about others' intentions or motivations. Additionally, emotions can affect the way individuals respond to feedback and criticism, with negative emotions often leading to defensive or avoidance behaviors.

Furthermore, emotions play a crucial role in the expression and communication of judgments. Individuals may convey their emotions through nonverbal cues such as facial expressions, gestures, and vocal intonation, which can influence how their judgments are received and interpreted by others. For example, a judgment expressed with anger or contempt may elicit defensive or hostile reactions from others, while a judgment conveyed with empathy or understanding may foster positive communication and mutual understanding.

In some cases, emotions can lead to cognitive biases and errors in judgment. For example, confirmation bias is the tendency to seek out information that confirms preexisting beliefs or emotional states, while the availability heuristic leads individuals to overestimate the likelihood of events that are more easily recalled due to their emotional salience. These biases can distort individuals' perceptions of reality and lead to irrational or unjustified judgments.

To mitigate the influence of emotions on judgment formation, individuals can practice emotional regulation and cognitive reappraisal techniques. Emotional regulation involves recognizing and managing one's emotional responses to situations, while cognitive reappraisal involves reframing the way one thinks about a situation to alter its emotional impact. By developing these skills, individuals can make more rational and objective judgments, free from the influence of fleeting emotional states.

In conclusion, the interplay of emotions in judgment formation is a complex and multifaceted phenomenon that shapes how individuals perceive, evaluate, and respond to the world around them. By understanding the role of emotions in judgment formation, individuals can develop greater self-awareness and emotional intelligence, leading to more informed and balanced decision-making processes.

Impact of Emotional Intelligence on Judgment

Emotional intelligence, often referred to as EQ, plays a crucial role in shaping how individuals form judgments and make decisions in various aspects of their lives. Unlike traditional measures of intelligence, which focus on cognitive abilities, emotional intelligence encompasses the ability to recognize, understand, and manage one's own emotions, as well as the ability to perceive and influence the emotions of others. Research suggests that individuals with higher levels of emotional intelligence tend to exhibit more balanced and effective judgment-making processes compared to those with lower levels of emotional intelligence.

One of the key ways in which emotional intelligence influences judgment is through self-awareness. Individuals with high emotional intelligence possess a strong understanding of their own emotions, including how their emotions influence their thoughts, behaviors, and decision-making processes. This self-awareness allows them to recognize when their emotions may be clouding their judgment and to take steps to manage those emotions effectively. For example, if faced with a challenging decision, someone with high emotional intelligence may take a step back to reflect on their emotional state before making a judgment, whereas someone with lower emotional intelligence may be more likely to react impulsively based on their immediate emotions.

Additionally, emotional intelligence enables individuals to accurately perceive and understand the emotions of others, which can also impact their judgment-making processes. This aspect of emotional intelligence, known as empathy, allows individuals to consider the perspectives and feelings of others when forming judgments or making decisions. For example, in a professional setting, someone with high emotional intelligence may take the time to listen to and understand the concerns of their colleagues before making a judgment about a particular issue. This ability to empathize with others can lead to more compassionate and equitable judgments.

Furthermore, individuals with high emotional intelligence are better equipped to manage interpersonal relationships and navigate social interactions effectively. This aspect of emotional intelligence, often referred to as social skills, allows individuals to communicate their judgments and decisions in a way that is respectful, diplomatic, and considerate of others' feelings. For example, when providing feedback or criticism, someone with high emotional intelligence may deliver their message in a constructive and empathetic manner, which can help to minimize conflict and promote understanding.

Moreover, emotional intelligence can also influence how individuals respond to feedback and criticism from others. Individuals with high emotional intelligence are more likely to view feedback as an opportunity for growth and self-improvement, rather than as a personal attack. This mindset allows them to learn from their mistakes and adjust their judgments and decision-making processes accordingly. On the other hand, individuals with lower emotional intelligence may be more defensive or resistant to feedback, which can hinder their ability to learn and grow.

In conclusion, emotional intelligence plays a significant role in shaping how individuals form judgments and make decisions in various aspects of their lives. By enhancing self-awareness, empathy, social skills, and the ability to manage emotions effectively, emotional intelligence enables individuals to make more balanced, thoughtful, and equitable judgments. As such, developing emotional intelligence can be beneficial for improving judgment-making processes and fostering positive interpersonal relationships in both personal and professional contexts.

The Role of Morality in Judgement

Morality, the principles that govern what is considered right and wrong, plays a significant role in shaping how individuals form judgments and make decisions in various aspects of their lives. Whether consciously or subconsciously, moral values influence individuals' perceptions of situations, their evaluations of others' actions, and the choices they ultimately make. Understanding the role of morality in judgment provides insight into the psychological processes underlying judgmental behavior.

At the core of moral judgment is the concept of ethical reasoning, which involves the application of moral principles to evaluate the morality of a given situation or action. Moral reasoning is influenced by a variety of factors, including cultural norms, personal beliefs, and social influences. Individuals may draw upon religious teachings, philosophical principles, or societal expectations to guide their moral judgments. For example, someone who values honesty as a moral principle may judge someone who lies more harshly than someone who does not place the same importance on honesty.

Additionally, moral judgment is closely tied to the emotions individuals experience when faced with moral dilemmas. Research in psychology has shown that moral judgments are often driven by emotions such as empathy, compassion, guilt, and indignation. These emotions serve as powerful motivators for moral behavior and can influence individuals' perceptions of right and wrong. For instance, witnessing an act of kindness may evoke feelings of warmth and admiration, leading to a positive moral judgment of the individual performing the act.

Moreover, moral judgment can be influenced by cognitive biases, which are systematic errors in thinking that can distort perceptions and lead to biased judgments. For example, confirmation bias, the tendency to search for, interpret, and recall information that confirms one's preexisting beliefs, can impact how individuals evaluate the morality of others' actions. Someone who holds a negative view of a particular group may be more likely to interpret their actions in a negative light, even if the evidence suggests otherwise.

Furthermore, moral judgment is influenced by social factors such as social norms, peer pressure, and group dynamics. Individuals may conform to the moral standards of their social group in order to gain acceptance and approval or avoid social rejection. This phenomenon, known as social conformity, can shape individuals' moral judgments and lead them to endorse beliefs and behaviors that align with the norms of their social environment.

Additionally, moral judgment is not always consistent across individuals or cultures. What one person considers morally acceptable may be viewed differently by another person or culture. These differences in moral judgment can lead to conflicts and disagreements, particularly in diverse societies where individuals hold varying cultural, religious, and ideological beliefs.

In conclusion, morality plays a fundamental role in shaping how individuals form judgments and make decisions in various aspects of their lives. Moral values, emotions, cognitive biases, and social factors all contribute to the complex process of moral judgment. Understanding the role of morality in judgment provides valuable insight into human behavior and helps to elucidate the psychological mechanisms underlying judgmental behavior.

Ethics and Judgment

Ethics and judgment are deeply intertwined concepts that shape individuals' perceptions, decisions, and behaviors in various aspects of life. Ethics refers to the principles that guide moral conduct and behavior, while judgment involves the process of evaluating situations, behaviors, and individuals based on one's beliefs, values, and perceptions. Understanding the relationship between ethics and judgment provides valuable insights into the psychological mechanisms underlying judgmental behavior.

One key aspect of the relationship between ethics and judgment is the role of moral principles in guiding individuals' evaluative processes. Ethical considerations often influence how individuals assess the morality of others' actions and behaviors. For example, someone who values honesty as a moral principle may judge someone who lies harshly, viewing their behavior as unethical or morally wrong. In this way, ethical principles serve as a framework for making moral judgments and evaluating the actions of oneself and others.

Furthermore, ethical judgment is influenced by a variety of factors, including personal beliefs, cultural norms, and societal expectations. Individuals may draw upon their ethical values and beliefs to guide their judgments and decisions in different situations. For instance, in a business context, ethical considerations may play a crucial role in decision-making processes, influencing how individuals assess the ethical implications of their actions and the potential consequences for themselves and others.

Moreover, ethical judgment is closely linked to empathy and compassion, which are essential components of ethical behavior. Empathy involves the ability to understand and share the feelings of others, while compassion involves a concern for the well-being of others and a desire to alleviate their suffering. These emotional responses play a vital role in shaping individuals' ethical judgments and influencing their decisions and actions. For example, individuals may be more likely to judge someone's behavior as unethical if they perceive it as causing harm or suffering to others.

Additionally, ethical judgment is influenced by cognitive biases, which are systematic errors in thinking that can distort perceptions and lead to biased judgments. For instance, confirmation bias, the tendency to search for, interpret, and recall information that confirms one's preexisting beliefs, can impact how individuals evaluate the ethicality of others' actions. Someone who holds a negative view of a particular group may be more likely to interpret their actions in a negative light, even if the evidence suggests otherwise.

Furthermore, ethical judgment is shaped by social factors such as social norms, peer pressure, and group dynamics. Individuals may conform to the ethical standards of their social group in order to gain acceptance and approval or avoid social rejection. This phenomenon, known as social conformity, can influence individuals' ethical judgments and lead them to endorse behaviors that align with the norms of their social environment.

In conclusion, ethics and judgment are closely intertwined concepts that play a fundamental role in shaping individuals' perceptions, decisions, and behaviors. Ethical principles, empathy, cognitive biases, and social factors all contribute to the complex process of ethical judgment. Understanding the relationship between ethics and judgment provides valuable insights into human behavior and helps to elucidate the psychological mechanisms underlying judgmental behavior.

Dynamics of Moral Judgments

Moral judgments are complex cognitive processes that involve evaluating the rightness or wrongness of actions based on ethical principles, cultural norms, personal beliefs, and situational factors. These judgments play a crucial role in guiding individuals' behavior and interactions with others, influencing how they navigate moral dilemmas and make decisions in various contexts.

One of the key dynamics of moral judgments is the interplay between individual beliefs and societal norms. Individuals develop their moral values and principles through a combination of personal experiences, cultural influences, and socialization processes. These beliefs serve as the foundation for moral judgments, shaping how individuals perceive and evaluate ethical dilemmas. However, societal norms also play a significant role in shaping moral judgments by providing guidelines for acceptable behavior within a given culture or community.

Furthermore, moral judgments are influenced by cognitive biases and heuristics, which are mental shortcuts that individuals use to make decisions more efficiently. These biases can lead to systematic errors in moral reasoning, affecting how individuals interpret moral situations and evaluate the actions of others. For example, the availability heuristic, which involves judging the likelihood of an event based on its ease of recall, can influence moral judgments by biasing individuals' perceptions of the prevalence of certain behaviors.

Moreover, emotional responses play a crucial role in moral judgments, influencing how individuals perceive and react to moral dilemmas. Emotions such as empathy, guilt, and disgust can shape individuals' moral judgments by influencing their emotional reactions to moral situations and guiding their decision-making processes. For example, individuals may judge an action as morally wrong if it elicits feelings of empathy for the victim or disgust at the perpetrator's behavior.

Additionally, moral judgments are subject to cultural variability, with different cultures and societies having distinct moral codes and ethical standards. What is considered morally acceptable in one culture may be viewed as morally reprehensible in another, highlighting the importance of cultural context in shaping moral judgments. Cross-cultural research has revealed differences in moral values and judgments across cultures, underscoring the role of cultural factors in influencing moral reasoning and decision-making.

Furthermore, moral judgments are often influenced by contextual factors, such as the perceived intentions of the actor, the consequences of the action, and the social context in which the behavior occurs. These situational factors can shape individuals' interpretations of moral situations and influence their moral judgments. For instance, individuals may judge an action as morally permissible if they believe it was motivated by good intentions, even if the outcome is negative.

In conclusion, the dynamics of moral judgments are shaped by a variety of factors, including individual beliefs, societal norms, cognitive biases, emotional responses, cultural influences, and situational factors. Understanding these dynamics provides valuable insights into the complexity of moral reasoning and decision-making processes. By examining the interplay between these factors, researchers can gain a deeper understanding of how moral judgments are formed and how they influence individuals' behavior in different contexts.

Psychological Challenges of Being Judgemental

Being judgmental is a cognitive and emotional process characterized by forming opinions or evaluations about others based on limited information, stereotypes, or personal biases. While making judgments is a natural aspect of human cognition, being excessively judgmental can lead to various psychological challenges for both the individual making the judgments and those being judged.

One of the primary psychological challenges of being judgmental is the tendency to engage in negative thinking patterns. When individuals habitually judge others, they often focus on perceived flaws or shortcomings, leading to a negative bias in their perceptions. This negative mindset can contribute to feelings of cynicism, hostility, and dissatisfaction with oneself and others, ultimately impacting overall mental well-being.

Furthermore, being judgmental can lead to the erosion of interpersonal relationships and social connections. Constantly critiquing and evaluating others can create an atmosphere of mistrust and hostility, making it difficult to form genuine connections with others. Individuals who are perceived as judgmental may struggle to maintain friendships or romantic relationships, as others may feel hesitant to open up or be themselves around them.

Moreover, being judgmental can perpetuate stereotypes and prejudice, contributing to the perpetuation of social inequalities and discrimination. When individuals make sweeping generalizations or assumptions about others based on superficial characteristics such as race, gender, or socioeconomic status, they reinforce harmful stereotypes and undermine efforts toward inclusivity and diversity. This can have profound psychological consequences for both the individuals being judged and the society as a whole, leading to feelings of alienation, marginalization, and injustice.

Another psychological challenge of being judgmental is the potential for cognitive dissonance and moral dilemmas. Individuals who hold rigid beliefs and judgments about others may experience cognitive dissonance when confronted with evidence that contradicts their preconceived notions. This internal conflict can lead to feelings of discomfort, guilt, or confusion as individuals grapple with reconciling their beliefs with reality. Additionally, being judgmental can create moral dilemmas for individuals who must navigate conflicting values or ethical principles, leading to internal conflict and moral distress.

Furthermore, being judgmental can hinder personal growth and self-awareness by preventing individuals from examining their own biases and shortcomings. When individuals are preoccupied with critiquing others, they may neglect self-reflection and introspection, missing opportunities for personal development and growth. This can lead to stagnation and a lack of emotional intelligence, as individuals fail to cultivate empathy, compassion, and self-awareness.

Overall, the psychological challenges of being judgmental are multifaceted and can have far-reaching consequences for individuals' mental well-being, interpersonal relationships, and societal dynamics. Overcoming these challenges requires individuals to cultivate self-awareness, empathy, and open-mindedness, challenging their own biases and assumptions while fostering a greater appreciation for diversity and complexity in human experience. By recognizing the detrimental effects of being judgmental and striving to cultivate a more compassionate and understanding mindset, individuals can promote greater psychological health and well-being for themselves and others.

Anxiety and Judgment

Anxiety and judgment often intertwine in complex ways, impacting individuals' mental well-being and social interactions. While judgment can trigger anxiety, anxiety can also exacerbate judgmental tendencies, creating a cycle of negative thoughts and behaviors.

One way in which anxiety influences judgment is by heightening individuals' sensitivity to perceived threats or social cues. When individuals experience anxiety, they may become hyper-aware of their surroundings and the behavior of others, leading to heightened vigilance and scrutiny. As a result, individuals may be more prone to making snap judgments or negative evaluations about others as a means of self-protection or threat avoidance.

Moreover, anxiety can distort individuals' perceptions of reality, leading to cognitive biases and irrational judgments. For example, individuals with social anxiety may catastrophize social interactions, interpreting neutral or ambiguous cues as signs of rejection or disapproval. This cognitive distortion can lead to excessive self-consciousness and self-criticism, as individuals become preoccupied with avoiding perceived judgment or embarrassment.

Additionally, anxiety can impair individuals' ability to accurately assess social situations and interpret others' intentions, leading to misinterpretations and misunderstandings. For instance, individuals with generalized anxiety disorder may perceive harmless comments or behaviors as threats or criticisms, leading to overreactive or defensive responses. This can strain interpersonal relationships and exacerbate feelings of isolation and loneliness.

Furthermore, anxiety can fuel perfectionistic tendencies and fear of failure, contributing to heightened judgmental attitudes toward oneself and others. Individuals with anxiety disorders may hold unrealistic standards for themselves and others, leading to chronic dissatisfaction and self-criticism. This perfectionistic mindset can also lead individuals to judge others harshly, as they project their own insecurities and fears onto those around them.

Conversely, judgmental attitudes can exacerbate anxiety symptoms by reinforcing negative thought patterns and self-doubt. When individuals engage in constant comparison or criticism of themselves and others, they perpetuate feelings of inadequacy and worthlessness, contributing to heightened anxiety and stress. Moreover, judgmental attitudes can create a cycle of rumination and worry, as individuals become preoccupied with past mistakes or perceived flaws.

In conclusion, the relationship between anxiety and judgment is multifaceted and bidirectional, with each influencing and reinforcing the other in complex ways. While anxiety can trigger judgmental tendencies through heightened sensitivity and cognitive distortions, judgmental attitudes can exacerbate anxiety symptoms by perpetuating negative thought patterns and self-criticism. Recognizing the interplay between anxiety and judgment is essential for promoting greater self-awareness and emotional well-being, as it allows individuals to identify and challenge maladaptive thought patterns and behaviors. By cultivating mindfulness, self-compassion, and empathy, individuals can reduce judgmental attitudes and alleviate anxiety, fostering greater psychological health and resilience.

Impact of Judgment on Self-Esteem

The impact of judgment on self-esteem is profound and can significantly affect individuals' psychological well-being. When individuals experience judgment from others or engage in self-judgment, it can lead to a range of negative outcomes, including lowered self-esteem, increased self-doubt, and diminished self-worth.

One way in which judgment affects self-esteem is through internalization. When individuals receive critical feedback or face judgment from others, they may internalize these negative evaluations, leading to feelings of inadequacy and unworthiness. For example, if someone receives harsh criticism from a peer or supervisor, they may begin to believe that they are not competent or capable, leading to a decline in self-esteem.

Moreover, repeated experiences of judgment can erode individuals' confidence and self-assurance over time. When individuals face consistent criticism or judgment, it can chip away at their sense of self-worth and undermine their belief in their abilities. This can create a cycle of self-doubt and negative self-talk, further reinforcing feelings of low self-esteem.

Furthermore, the fear of judgment can inhibit individuals from pursuing their goals or expressing themselves authentically. When individuals are overly concerned about how they will be perceived by others, they may avoid taking risks or putting themselves in vulnerable situations, leading to missed opportunities for growth and self-expression. This can perpetuate feelings of stagnation and dissatisfaction, further contributing to diminished self-esteem.

Additionally, self-judgment can be a significant source of low self-esteem. When individuals engage in negative self-talk or hold themselves to unrealistic standards, it can lead to feelings of shame, guilt, and self-blame. For example, if someone constantly criticizes themselves for their perceived flaws or mistakes, it can undermine their self-confidence and self-worth, leading to a downward spiral of negative self-esteem.

Moreover, comparison plays a significant role in the impact of judgment on self-esteem. When individuals compare themselves to others and perceive themselves as falling short, it can lead to feelings of inferiority and inadequacy. Social media and other forms of media often exacerbate this tendency, as individuals are bombarded with images and messages that promote unrealistic standards of beauty, success, and happiness. This constant comparison can fuel feelings of insecurity and self-doubt, further contributing to diminished self-esteem.

In conclusion, the impact of judgment on self-esteem is significant and multifaceted. Whether it comes from external sources or internal self-talk, judgment can erode individuals' confidence, self-worth, and sense of identity. Recognizing the influence of judgment on self-esteem is essential for promoting greater self-awareness and resilience. By challenging negative thought patterns, practicing self-compassion, and seeking support from others, individuals can cultivate a healthier relationship with themselves and bolster their self-esteem.

Judgment and Interpersonal Relationships

Judgment plays a pivotal role in interpersonal relationships, influencing how individuals perceive, interact with, and relate to others. While judgment can serve as a mechanism for evaluating situations and making decisions, it can also have significant implications for the dynamics and outcomes of interpersonal interactions.

One aspect of judgment in interpersonal relationships is its impact on communication. When individuals engage in judgmental behaviors, such as criticizing, blaming, or making assumptions about others, it can lead to breakdowns in communication and misunderstandings. For example, if one partner in a romantic relationship constantly judges the other's actions or decisions, it can create feelings of defensiveness and resentment, hindering effective communication and connection.

Moreover, judgment can shape the quality and depth of relationships. When individuals feel judged or criticized by others, it can erode trust and intimacy, leading to feelings of alienation and disconnection. In contrast, when individuals feel accepted, understood, and supported by others, it fosters feelings of safety and belonging, strengthening the bond between them. Therefore, judgment can either enhance or undermine the overall quality of interpersonal relationships.

Furthermore, judgment can influence individuals' perceptions of themselves and others within the context of relationships. When individuals feel judged by their peers, friends, or romantic partners, it can impact their self-esteem and self-worth, leading to feelings of insecurity and inadequacy. Similarly, when individuals judge others harshly or unfairly, it can create distance and strain in relationships, as the judged individual may feel misunderstood or devalued.

Additionally, judgment can contribute to conflict and tension in interpersonal relationships. When individuals impose their own beliefs, values, or expectations onto others and judge them for not meeting these standards, it can lead to disagreements and power struggles. For example, if one colleague judges another for their work style or approach, it can create friction and animosity in the workplace, impacting productivity and morale.

Moreover, judgment can influence individuals' willingness to be vulnerable and authentic in relationships. When individuals fear being judged or rejected by others, they may withhold parts of themselves or put up emotional barriers as a form of self-protection. This can prevent genuine connection and intimacy from developing, as individuals may struggle to express their true thoughts, feelings, and needs.

Furthermore, judgment can perpetuate stereotypes and biases in interpersonal relationships. When individuals make assumptions or judgments based on superficial characteristics such as race, gender, or appearance, it can lead to discrimination and prejudice. This can create barriers to meaningful interaction and understanding, as individuals may be quick to judge others based on preconceived notions rather than taking the time to get to know them as individuals.

In conclusion, judgment has profound implications for interpersonal relationships, shaping how individuals communicate, relate to others, and perceive themselves and others. By fostering empathy, open-mindedness, and acceptance, individuals can cultivate healthier and more fulfilling relationships based on mutual respect, understanding, and support.

Effects of Judgments on Relationships

Judgments, whether implicit or explicit, can significantly impact relationships in various ways, shaping how individuals perceive themselves and others within the context of social interactions. These effects can be both positive and negative, influencing the dynamics and outcomes of relationships.

One notable effect of judgments on relationships is the creation of emotional distance and disconnection between individuals. When one person feels judged or criticized by another, it can lead to feelings of resentment, defensiveness, and alienation. This can create a barrier to open communication and authentic expression, hindering the development of trust and intimacy in the relationship.

Moreover, judgments can contribute to a breakdown in empathy and understanding between individuals. When someone is quick to judge another without considering their perspective or experiences, it can lead to misunderstandings and misinterpretations. This lack of empathy can strain the relationship and prevent meaningful connection from forming, as individuals may feel misunderstood or invalidated by the judgments of others.

Additionally, judgments can impact individuals' self-esteem and self-worth within relationships. When someone is subjected to harsh or unfair judgments by their partner, friend, or family member, it can erode their confidence and sense of value. This can lead to feelings of insecurity and inadequacy, undermining the individual's ability to assert themselves and advocate for their needs within the relationship.

Furthermore, judgments can fuel resentment and conflict in relationships, particularly when they are perceived as unjust or unwarranted. When individuals feel unfairly judged or criticized by their partner or loved one, it can lead to arguments, tension, and hostility. This can create a negative cycle of blame and defensiveness, further damaging the relationship and eroding trust and goodwill between individuals.

On the other hand, judgments can also serve as a catalyst for personal growth and development within relationships. When individuals receive constructive feedback or criticism from their partner or loved one, it can provide valuable insights and opportunities for self-reflection and improvement. This can foster greater self-awareness and empathy, strengthening the bond between individuals and promoting mutual growth and understanding.

Moreover, judgments can help individuals establish boundaries and clarify their values and priorities within relationships. When someone recognizes and communicates their boundaries and expectations to their partner or loved one, it can promote respect, trust, and mutual understanding. This can create a healthier and more balanced dynamic in the relationship, fostering a sense of security and stability for both individuals involved.

In conclusion, judgments have profound effects on relationships, influencing how individuals perceive themselves and others, communicate, and interact within social contexts. By fostering empathy, open-mindedness, and constructive communication, individuals can navigate judgments more effectively and cultivate healthier and more fulfilling relationships based on mutual respect, understanding, and support.

Strategies of Managing Judgment in Relationships

In navigating the complex landscape of relationships, managing judgments—both those we receive and those we impose—is crucial for fostering understanding, empathy, and mutual respect. Several strategies can help individuals effectively manage judgment in their relationships, promoting healthier dynamics and stronger connections.

Firstly, practicing self-awareness is essential in managing judgments within relationships. By becoming mindful of our own biases, insecurities, and triggers, we can better understand how they influence our perceptions and interactions with others. Engaging in self-reflection and introspection allows individuals to recognize when they are projecting their own judgments onto others and empowers them to take responsibility for their thoughts and actions.

Communication also plays a vital role in managing judgment within relationships. Open and honest dialogue allows individuals to express their feelings, concerns, and perspectives without fear of judgment or criticism. By fostering a safe and non-judgmental environment for communication, individuals can address misunderstandings, resolve conflicts, and strengthen their connection with their partner or loved one.

Moreover, practicing empathy is essential in managing judgment within relationships. Empathy involves actively listening to others, seeking to understand their experiences, and validating their emotions without judgment. By putting ourselves in the shoes of our partner or loved one, we can gain insight into their perspective and cultivate greater compassion and understanding in our interactions.

Setting boundaries is another crucial strategy for managing judgment in relationships. Establishing clear boundaries helps individuals protect their emotional well-being and maintain a sense of autonomy and self-respect. By communicating their boundaries assertively and respectfully, individuals can mitigate the risk of judgmental behavior and create a healthier and more balanced dynamic in the relationship.

Furthermore, practicing forgiveness and acceptance is key in managing judgment within relationships. Forgiveness involves letting go of resentment and releasing the desire for revenge or retribution. Acceptance, on the other hand, involves embracing others for who they are, flaws and all, without trying to change or control them. By practicing forgiveness and acceptance, individuals can foster greater compassion, empathy, and understanding in their relationships, creating space for growth and reconciliation.

Cultivating a growth mindset is also essential in managing judgment within relationships. A growth mindset involves believing that individuals have the capacity to learn, grow, and change over time. By adopting a growth mindset, individuals can view judgment as an opportunity for personal and relational growth rather than a fixed reflection of their character or worth. This perspective encourages individuals to approach conflicts and challenges with curiosity, resilience, and a willingness to learn from their experiences.

Finally, seeking support from trusted friends, family members, or mental health professionals can be invaluable in managing judgment within relationships. Talking to others who can offer perspective, guidance, and support can help individuals process their emotions, gain insight into their relationships, and develop effective coping strategies for managing judgmental behavior.

In conclusion, managing judgment within relationships requires self-awareness, effective communication, empathy, boundary-setting, forgiveness, acceptance, a growth mindset, and support from others. By employing these strategies, individuals can navigate judgmental behavior more effectively and cultivate healthier, more fulfilling relationships based on mutual respect, understanding, and compassion.

Cultural Influence on Judgement

Cultural influence plays a significant role in shaping how individuals perceive and judge the world around them. These cultural norms, values, and beliefs influence the way people interpret behaviors, make decisions, and form opinions about others. Understanding the cultural context is essential in comprehending the psychology of being judgmental.

Cultural influence on judgment begins with socialization, where individuals learn the norms and values of their culture through family, education, media, and social interactions. These cultural norms shape people's perceptions of what is considered acceptable or unacceptable behavior, influencing how they judge others based on these standards.

In collectivist cultures, such as many Asian and African societies, the emphasis is on group harmony and conformity to social norms. As a result, individuals from these cultures may be more inclined to judge others based on their adherence to societal expectations and norms. Conversely, in individualistic cultures like those found in Western societies, there is a greater emphasis on personal autonomy and individual achievement. People from these cultures may be more likely to judge others based on their individual accomplishments and personal characteristics.

Cultural values also play a significant role in shaping judgment. For example, cultures that prioritize hierarchy and authority may lead individuals to judge others based on their perceived status or social standing. In contrast, cultures that emphasize egalitarianism and equality may lead individuals to judge others based on their fairness and justice.

Moreover, cultural beliefs and stereotypes can influence judgment by creating biases and prejudices against certain groups of people. These stereotypes are often based on cultural representations in media, literature, and popular culture, which can perpetuate negative perceptions and attitudes towards particular ethnic, racial, or social groups. These biases can lead to discriminatory behavior and unfair treatment of others based on their cultural background.

Cultural differences in communication styles can also impact judgment. For example, cultures that value direct and assertive communication may perceive indirect or nonverbal communication as dishonest or deceptive. Conversely, cultures that prioritize indirect communication may view direct communication as rude or confrontational.

These differences in communication styles can lead to misunderstandings and misinterpretations, which can influence judgment and perception of others.

Furthermore, cultural norms regarding emotions and expression can influence judgment. In some cultures, emotional expression is encouraged and seen as a sign of authenticity and sincerity. In contrast, in other cultures, emotional restraint and composure are valued, and overt displays of emotion may be viewed as weak or unprofessional. These cultural differences can affect how individuals judge others based on their emotional expression and behavior.

In conclusion, cultural influence plays a significant role in shaping judgment and perception of others. Cultural norms, values, beliefs, stereotypes, communication styles, and attitudes towards emotions all contribute to how individuals form opinions and make judgments about others. Understanding these cultural influences is essential in promoting cultural competence, empathy, and understanding in interpersonal interactions.

Cultural Norms and Judgment

Cultural norms play a significant role in shaping the way individuals perceive and judge the behaviors of others. These norms are the unwritten rules and expectations that govern social interactions within a particular culture. Understanding cultural norms is essential in comprehending the psychology of being judgmental.

One aspect of cultural norms that influences judgment is the concept of etiquette and politeness. Different cultures have varying expectations regarding appropriate behavior in social situations. For example, in some cultures, it is considered polite to maintain direct eye contact during conversations, while in others, it may be seen as disrespectful or confrontational. These cultural differences in etiquette can lead individuals to judge others based on their adherence to these norms.

Moreover, cultural norms dictate what is considered acceptable or unacceptable behavior within a society. For instance, in some cultures, punctuality is highly valued, and being late for appointments or meetings is frowned upon. In contrast, in other cultures, a more relaxed attitude towards time may be prevalent. Individuals from these cultures may judge others based on their adherence to these cultural norms regarding punctuality.

Cultural norms also influence gender roles and expectations, which can impact judgment. For example, in traditional societies, there may be specific roles and responsibilities assigned to men and women based on their gender. Individuals who deviate from these gender norms may be judged harshly by others. Similarly, cultural norms surrounding masculinity and femininity can influence how individuals judge others based on their adherence to these gender norms.

Additionally, cultural norms regarding social hierarchy and status can influence judgment. In societies where hierarchy is highly valued, individuals may judge others based on their perceived social status or position within the hierarchy. This can lead to discrimination and prejudice against those perceived as being of lower status.

Cultural norms also shape attitudes towards authority and obedience. In some cultures, respect for authority figures is highly valued, and individuals may be judged based on their deference to authority. In contrast, in cultures that value individual autonomy and independence, excessive deference to authority may be viewed negatively.

Furthermore, cultural norms regarding personal space and physical contact can influence judgment. In some cultures, such as those in Southern Europe or Latin America, physical contact such as hugging or kissing on the cheek is common in social interactions. In contrast, in cultures that value personal space, such behavior may be seen as intrusive or inappropriate. Individuals from these cultures may judge others based on their comfort level with physical contact.

In conclusion, cultural norms play a crucial role in shaping judgment and perception of others. These norms influence expectations regarding etiquette, behavior, gender roles, social hierarchy, authority, and personal space. Understanding cultural norms is essential in promoting cultural competence and reducing misunderstandings and misinterpretations in interpersonal interactions. By recognizing and respecting cultural differences, individuals can foster greater empathy, understanding, and acceptance of others.

Comparative Analysis of Judgment Across Cultures

Judgment is a complex psychological process influenced by various factors, including cultural norms, values, and beliefs. When examining judgment across cultures, it becomes evident that different societies have distinct approaches to evaluating behaviors, actions, and individuals. A comparative analysis of judgment across cultures reveals both similarities and differences, highlighting the intricate interplay between culture and psychology.

One aspect of judgment that varies across cultures is the perception of individualism versus collectivism. In individualistic cultures such as the United States and Western Europe, emphasis is placed on personal achievement, autonomy, and self-expression. In contrast, collectivist cultures, such as those in East Asia and Africa, prioritize group harmony, interdependence, and social cohesion. Consequently, individuals from individualistic cultures may be more inclined to make judgments based on personal attributes and achievements, whereas those from collectivist cultures may focus on social relationships and group dynamics.

Moreover, cultural values influence the criteria used to evaluate behaviors and actions. For example, in cultures that prioritize egalitarianism and fairness, individuals may be judged based on their adherence to principles of equality and justice. In contrast, in hierarchical cultures, individuals may be judged based on their perceived status, power, or authority. Additionally, cultural attitudes towards risk-taking, innovation, and conformity can impact judgment. In cultures that value risk-taking and innovation, individuals may be praised for taking bold initiatives, whereas in cultures that emphasize conformity, deviation from social norms may be viewed negatively.

Cultural norms regarding communication styles also influence judgment. In some cultures, direct communication is valued, and individuals may be judged based on their ability to express themselves clearly and assertively. In contrast, in cultures that favor indirect communication, individuals may be judged based on their sensitivity to social cues and nonverbal signals. Moreover, attitudes towards conflict resolution and negotiation vary across cultures, affecting how individuals are judged in interpersonal conflicts.

Furthermore, cultural attitudes towards time can impact judgment. In cultures that value punctuality and efficiency, individuals may be judged based on their timeliness and productivity. In contrast, in cultures with a more relaxed attitude towards time, such as some Latin American and African cultures, individuals may be judged based on their ability to prioritize relationships and adapt to changing circumstances.

Religious and spiritual beliefs also play a significant role in shaping judgment across cultures. In cultures where religion holds significant influence, individuals may be judged based on their adherence to religious teachings and moral principles. Moreover, cultural attitudes towards moral virtues and vices can vary based on religious beliefs, affecting how individuals are perceived and judged by others.

In conclusion, a comparative analysis of judgment across cultures reveals the intricate relationship between culture and psychology. Cultural norms, values, and beliefs shape the criteria used to evaluate behaviors, actions, and individuals. Understanding these cultural differences is essential for promoting cross-cultural understanding, empathy, and effective communication. By recognizing and respecting cultural diversity, individuals can develop more nuanced perspectives and mitigate the impact of cultural biases on judgment.

Overcoming Judgmental Behavior

Overcoming judgmental behavior is a multifaceted process that requires self-awareness, empathy, and a willingness to challenge ingrained beliefs and biases. Judgmental behavior stems from various psychological factors, including cognitive biases, social conditioning, and emotional responses. By understanding the psychology behind judgmental behavior, individuals can take proactive steps to cultivate empathy, open-mindedness, and acceptance.

One of the key factors contributing to judgmental behavior is cognitive biases. These biases are mental shortcuts that the brain uses to process information quickly, but they can also lead to distorted perceptions and judgments. For example, confirmation bias causes individuals to seek out information that confirms their existing beliefs while ignoring evidence that contradicts them. Overcoming cognitive biases requires conscious effort and critical thinking skills. By actively questioning assumptions and seeking out diverse perspectives, individuals can challenge their ingrained biases and develop a more balanced and nuanced understanding of the world.

Social conditioning also plays a significant role in shaping judgmental behavior. From a young age, individuals are exposed to societal norms, cultural values, and media portrayals that influence their perceptions of others. Stereotypes, prejudices, and discriminatory attitudes are often reinforced through socialization processes, leading to judgmental behavior towards individuals who deviate from societal norms or belong to marginalized groups. Overcoming social conditioning requires introspection and education. By examining the origins of their beliefs and questioning societal norms, individuals can challenge stereotypes and cultivate empathy towards others.

Emotional responses also contribute to judgmental behavior. When individuals feel threatened, insecure, or vulnerable, they may resort to judgment as a defense mechanism to protect themselves. For example, feelings of envy or insecurity may lead individuals to judge others harshly in an attempt to boost their own self-esteem. Overcoming judgmental behavior requires emotional regulation and self-reflection. By acknowledging and processing their emotions in healthy ways, individuals can develop greater emotional resilience and empathy towards others.

One effective strategy for overcoming judgmental behavior is practicing mindfulness. Mindfulness involves cultivating present moment awareness and nonjudgmental acceptance of thoughts, feelings, and experiences. By observing their thoughts without attaching judgment or criticism, individuals can gain insight into their underlying biases and assumptions. Mindfulness also helps individuals develop greater empathy and compassion towards others by fostering a deeper understanding of shared humanity and interconnectedness.

Another strategy for overcoming judgmental behavior is fostering empathy through perspective-taking exercises. Perspective-taking involves imagining oneself in another person's shoes and considering their thoughts, feelings, and experiences. By empathizing with others and seeing the world from their perspective, individuals can develop greater compassion and understanding. Engaging in meaningful conversations with individuals from diverse backgrounds and actively listening to their experiences can also help challenge stereotypes and broaden one's worldview.

In conclusion, overcoming judgmental behavior is a complex but achievable process that requires self-awareness, empathy, and a commitment to personal growth. By understanding the psychological factors that contribute to judgmental behavior and implementing strategies such as mindfulness, perspective-taking, and education, individuals can cultivate greater empathy, open-mindedness, and acceptance towards others. Through continuous self-reflection and conscious effort, individuals can contribute to creating a more compassionate and inclusive society.

Methods of Reducing Judgemental Behavior

Reducing judgmental behavior requires a concerted effort to understand the psychological mechanisms behind it and implement effective strategies for change. There are several methods individuals can employ to diminish their propensity for judgment and foster a more open-minded and empathetic outlook.

One method of reducing judgmental behavior is through self-awareness and introspection. Individuals can start by reflecting on their own thoughts, feelings, and biases, and examining how these factors influence their perceptions of others. By recognizing and acknowledging their own prejudices and assumptions, individuals can begin to challenge them and cultivate a more objective and empathetic perspective.

Another effective method is practicing empathy and perspective-taking. Empathy involves putting oneself in another person's shoes and understanding their thoughts, feelings, and experiences. By actively listening to others, seeking to understand their perspectives, and showing compassion for their struggles, individuals can develop greater empathy and reduce the tendency to judge.

Mindfulness meditation is also a powerful tool for reducing judgmental behavior. Mindfulness involves paying attention to the present moment with openness, curiosity, and acceptance. Through regular mindfulness practice, individuals can learn to observe their thoughts and emotions without attaching judgment or criticism, allowing them to respond to situations with greater clarity and equanimity.

Education and exposure to diversity are essential for reducing judgmental behavior. By learning about different cultures, beliefs, and lived experiences, individuals can broaden their understanding of the world and challenge stereotypes and prejudices. Engaging in meaningful conversations with people from diverse backgrounds and actively seeking out diverse perspectives can help individuals expand their worldview and reduce the tendency to judge others based on superficial characteristics.

Developing critical thinking skills is another important method for reducing judgmental behavior. Critical thinking involves evaluating information objectively, questioning assumptions, and considering evidence before forming opinions or making judgments. By honing their critical thinking skills, individuals can become more discerning and less susceptible to biased or prejudiced thinking.

Practicing gratitude and focusing on positive aspects of others can also help reduce judgmental behavior. Gratitude involves acknowledging and appreciating the good qualities in others, rather than focusing solely on their flaws or shortcomings. By cultivating a mindset of gratitude and appreciation, individuals can foster empathy and compassion towards others, reducing the inclination to judge.

Finally, seeking feedback from others and being open to constructive criticism can help individuals identify and address their own biases and blind spots. By soliciting feedback from trusted friends, family members, or colleagues, individuals can gain valuable insights into their own behavior and attitudes, allowing them to make positive changes and become more inclusive and accepting of others.

In conclusion, reducing judgmental behavior requires a combination of self-awareness, empathy, critical thinking, and exposure to diversity. By practicing mindfulness, empathy, gratitude, and critical thinking, individuals can cultivate a more open-minded and compassionate approach to others, leading to stronger relationships, greater understanding, and a more harmonious society.

Practices for Nurturing Non-judgmental Thinking

Nurturing non-judgmental thinking is essential for fostering empathy, understanding, and harmonious relationships with others. Here are several effective practices that can help individuals cultivate a mindset of non-judgment:

Mindfulness Meditation: Mindfulness meditation involves paying attention to the present moment with openness, curiosity, and acceptance. By practicing mindfulness, individuals can learn to observe their thoughts and emotions without attaching judgment or criticism. Regular meditation can help quiet the mind, increase self-awareness, and promote non-judgmental thinking.

Self-Reflection: Taking time for self-reflection allows individuals to examine their thoughts, feelings, and behaviors without judgment. Through journaling, introspection, or therapy, individuals can explore their own biases, assumptions, and triggers. By gaining insight into their own thought patterns, individuals can begin to challenge and change judgmental tendencies.

Empathy Building Exercises: Engaging in empathy-building exercises can help individuals develop greater compassion and understanding towards others. Role-playing, perspective-taking activities, or volunteering in the community can provide opportunities to see the world from different viewpoints. By putting themselves in another person's shoes, individuals can foster empathy and reduce the inclination to judge.

Cultivating Gratitude: Practicing gratitude involves acknowledging and appreciating the positive aspects of life and other people. By focusing on what they are grateful for, individuals can shift their perspective away from judgment and towards appreciation. Keeping a gratitude journal, expressing gratitude to others, or simply pausing to reflect on blessings can help cultivate a mindset of non-judgment.

Open-Mindedness: Cultivating open-mindedness involves being receptive to new ideas, perspectives, and experiences. Individuals can challenge themselves to seek out diverse viewpoints, engage in respectful dialogue with others, and approach situations with curiosity rather than preconceived notions. By remaining open-minded, individuals can expand their understanding and reduce the tendency to judge.

Practice Non-Attachment: Non-attachment involves letting go of rigid expectations, preferences, and attachments to outcomes. By practicing non-attachment, individuals can approach situations with greater flexibility and acceptance, reducing the tendency to judge when things do not go as planned. Letting go of the need to control or impose one's own beliefs onto others can foster a more non-judgmental attitude.

Mindful Communication: Practicing mindful communication involves speaking and listening with awareness, intention, and compassion. By paying attention to their words and how they impact others, individuals can communicate more effectively and avoid making hasty judgments. Active listening, empathy, and non-verbal cues can help promote understanding and reduce judgment in interpersonal interactions.

Educating Oneself: Increasing awareness and understanding of social issues, diversity, and human behavior can help individuals challenge stereotypes and prejudices. Reading books, attending workshops, or participating in diversity training programs can provide valuable insights and perspectives. By learning about different cultures, experiences, and perspectives, individuals can cultivate empathy and reduce judgmental thinking.

In conclusion, nurturing non-judgmental thinking requires self-awareness, empathy, open-mindedness, and intentional effort. By practicing mindfulness, empathy-building exercises, gratitude, and non-attachment, individuals can cultivate a mindset of acceptance, understanding, and compassion towards themselves and others. Mindful communication and ongoing education can further support the development of non-judgmental thinking, leading to stronger relationships, greater empathy, and a more inclusive and compassionate society.

The Role of Empathy in Non-judgment

Empathy plays a crucial role in fostering non-judgmental attitudes and behaviors towards others. It involves the ability to understand and share the feelings, perspectives, and experiences of others, which in turn promotes compassion, understanding, and acceptance. In the context of the psychology of being judgmental, empathy serves as a powerful antidote to prejudice, bias, and stereotyping.

Empathy enables individuals to see the world from different perspectives, allowing them to recognize the humanity and complexity of others. By putting themselves in another person's shoes, individuals can better understand the factors that shape someone's thoughts, feelings, and behaviors, leading to greater empathy and reduced judgment.

One way empathy promotes non-judgment is by helping individuals recognize the common humanity they share with others. When people empathize with others, they acknowledge that everyone experiences pain, joy, and challenges in life. This recognition of shared humanity can break down barriers and foster a sense of connection and solidarity, reducing the inclination to judge others based on superficial differences.

Furthermore, empathy allows individuals to suspend their own biases and assumptions, creating space for genuine understanding and acceptance. Rather than imposing their own perspectives onto others, empathetic individuals seek to listen, validate, and support others' experiences, even if they differ from their own. This willingness to listen and learn from others promotes non-judgmental attitudes and fosters deeper connections and relationships.

Empathy also serves as a catalyst for behavior change by motivating individuals to take compassionate action. When people empathize with others who are experiencing hardship or injustice, they are more likely to advocate for positive change and support initiatives that promote equality, justice, and inclusion. By actively working to address systemic issues and support marginalized communities, empathetic individuals contribute to a more empathetic and non-judgmental society.

Moreover, empathy promotes effective communication and conflict resolution by encouraging individuals to approach differences with curiosity and understanding rather than judgment and defensiveness. When people empathize with others' perspectives, they can engage in constructive dialogue, find common ground, and resolve conflicts peacefully. This empathetic approach to communication fosters mutual respect, trust, and collaboration, ultimately strengthening relationships and communities.

It's important to note that empathy is not synonymous with agreement or condoning harmful behavior. Instead, empathy involves acknowledging and validating others' experiences while holding them accountable for their actions. By empathizing with someone's feelings or struggles, individuals can offer support and understanding without necessarily endorsing their behavior.

In conclusion, empathy plays a vital role in promoting non-judgmental attitudes and behaviors towards others. By fostering understanding, compassion, and connection, empathy breaks down barriers, reduces prejudice, and promotes positive social change. As individuals cultivate empathy in their interactions and relationships, they contribute to a more empathetic, inclusive, and non-judgmental society where everyone feels seen, heard, and valued.

Understanding Empathy

Empathy is a fundamental aspect of human psychology that involves the ability to understand and share the feelings, thoughts, and experiences of others. It plays a crucial role in interpersonal relationships, social interactions, and emotional intelligence. In the context of the psychology of being judgmental, empathy serves as a powerful tool for fostering understanding, compassion, and acceptance towards others.

Empathy consists of several components, including cognitive empathy, emotional empathy, and compassionate empathy. Cognitive empathy involves the ability to understand and recognize the thoughts, perspectives, and intentions of others. It requires individuals to put themselves in someone else's shoes and consider the world from their perspective. Emotional empathy, on the other hand, involves experiencing and sharing the emotions of others. It allows individuals to resonate with someone else's feelings and respond with appropriate emotional reactions. Lastly, compassionate empathy combines cognitive and emotional empathy with a desire to alleviate the suffering or distress of others. It motivates individuals to take action and offer support to those in need.

Research has shown that empathy is a complex psychological phenomenon influenced by various factors, including genetics, upbringing, and socialization. Some individuals may naturally possess higher levels of empathy due to genetic predispositions or early childhood experiences, while others may develop empathy through exposure to diverse perspectives and experiences. Additionally, cultural and societal norms play a significant role in shaping individuals' empathetic responses and behaviors. For example, cultures that prioritize collectivism and interdependence may emphasize empathy and compassion towards others, while cultures that value individualism may prioritize self-interest and autonomy.

Empathy has profound implications for personal relationships, social dynamics, and mental well-being. In interpersonal relationships, empathy enhances communication, trust, and intimacy by fostering mutual understanding and validation. When individuals feel heard, understood, and supported by others, they are more likely to develop meaningful connections and build strong bonds. Empathetic responses also contribute to conflict resolution and problem-solving by promoting active listening, empathy, and perspective-taking. By understanding and validating each other's perspectives, individuals can find common ground and work towards mutually beneficial solutions.

Furthermore, empathy plays a crucial role in social interactions and community cohesion. It promotes prosocial behaviors, such as kindness, generosity, and cooperation, by encouraging individuals to consider the needs and feelings of others. Empathetic individuals are more likely to engage in altruistic acts and support initiatives that promote social justice, equality, and inclusivity. In diverse and multicultural societies, empathy serves as a bridge that connects people from different backgrounds and fosters understanding and acceptance across cultural divides.

From a psychological perspective, empathy is closely linked to emotional intelligence, mental health, and overall well-being. Studies have shown that individuals with higher levels of empathy tend to have better mental health outcomes, including lower levels of stress, anxiety, and depression. Empathetic individuals are also more resilient in the face of adversity and better equipped to navigate challenging situations. By fostering empathy in ourselves and others, we can promote psychological resilience, emotional regulation, and positive mental health outcomes.

In conclusion, empathy is a multifaceted psychological phenomenon that plays a crucial role in human relationships, social interactions, and emotional well-being. It involves the ability to understand, share, and respond to the feelings and experiences of others with compassion and kindness. By cultivating empathy in ourselves and fostering empathetic attitudes and behaviors in our communities, we can create a more compassionate, understanding, and inclusive society where everyone feels valued and supported.

Empathetic Interaction to Counter Judgment

Empathetic interaction serves as a potent antidote to the toxic effects of judgmental behavior, offering a pathway towards greater understanding, compassion, and connection in interpersonal relationships and social dynamics. In the realm of psychology, the practice of empathetic interaction is crucial for fostering empathy, promoting emotional intelligence, and mitigating the harmful consequences of being judgmental.

At its core, empathetic interaction involves the ability to engage with others in a way that demonstrates empathy, understanding, and validation of their experiences and perspectives. It requires individuals to actively listen, acknowledge, and empathize with the thoughts, feelings, and needs of others without passing judgment or criticism. By adopting an empathetic stance, individuals can create a safe and supportive environment where open communication, mutual respect, and emotional vulnerability are encouraged.

One of the key components of empathetic interaction is active listening. Active listening involves giving full attention to the speaker, maintaining eye contact, and providing verbal and nonverbal cues to signal understanding and empathy. It requires individuals to set aside their own preconceptions and judgments and focus on truly understanding the speaker's point of view. By listening attentively and empathetically, individuals can validate the speaker's experiences and emotions, fostering a sense of trust and rapport in the relationship.

Another essential aspect of empathetic interaction is perspective-taking. Perspective-taking involves imagining oneself in the shoes of another person and considering the world from their viewpoint. It requires individuals to step outside of their own biases, assumptions, and beliefs and empathize with the experiences and perspectives of others. By engaging in perspective-taking, individuals can develop a deeper understanding of others' motivations, emotions, and behaviors, promoting empathy and compassion in their interactions.

Furthermore, empathetic interaction involves validating the emotions and experiences of others without judgment or criticism. Validation entails acknowledging and accepting the validity of someone else's feelings, even if they differ from one's own. It requires individuals to demonstrate empathy and understanding towards others' emotional experiences, providing validation and support without minimizing or invalidating their feelings. By validating others' emotions, individuals can foster trust, intimacy, and connection in their relationships.

Empathetic interaction also plays a crucial role in conflict resolution and problem-solving. In situations of conflict or disagreement, empathetic communication can help de-escalate tensions and facilitate constructive dialogue. By listening empathetically to each other's perspectives, individuals can identify common ground, explore alternative solutions, and work towards mutually satisfactory outcomes. Empathetic interaction promotes collaboration, compromise, and reconciliation, fostering healthier and more harmonious relationships.

Moreover, empathetic interaction contributes to the cultivation of emotional intelligence, resilience, and well-being. Research has shown that individuals who engage in empathetic communication tend to have higher levels of emotional intelligence, including self-awareness, self-regulation, and social skills. Empathetic individuals are better able to navigate complex social dynamics, manage interpersonal conflicts, and build meaningful connections with others. By practicing empathetic interaction, individuals can enhance their emotional resilience, promote mental health, and cultivate a more compassionate and empathetic society.

In conclusion, empathetic interaction serves as a powerful tool for countering judgmental behavior and promoting empathy, understanding, and connection in interpersonal relationships and social interactions. By actively listening, perspective-taking, validating others' emotions, and fostering constructive dialogue, individuals can create a supportive and inclusive environment where empathy and compassion thrive. Empathetic interaction contributes to the development of emotional intelligence, conflict resolution skills, and psychological well-being, making it an essential practice in the psychology of being non-judgmental.

Understanding and Dealing with Judgemental People

Understanding and dealing with judgmental people can be a challenging yet important aspect of navigating social interactions and maintaining emotional well-being. In the realm of psychology, it is essential to explore the underlying factors that contribute to judgmental behavior and develop effective strategies for managing and responding to it.

Firstly, it is crucial to understand that judgmental behavior often stems from deep-seated insecurities, biases, and cognitive biases. Individuals who exhibit judgmental tendencies may do so as a way to validate their own beliefs or bolster their self-esteem. They may project their own fears and insecurities onto others, using judgment as a defense mechanism to protect themselves from feelings of vulnerability or inadequacy. By recognizing the underlying motivations behind judgmental behavior, individuals can cultivate empathy and understanding towards judgmental people, rather than reacting defensively or reciprocating with judgment of their own.

Moreover, it is essential to practice self-awareness and emotional regulation when dealing with judgmental people. Recognizing one's own triggers and emotional responses to judgmental behavior can help individuals maintain composure and respond in a calm and assertive manner. Instead of internalizing or reacting defensively to judgments, individuals can choose to set healthy boundaries, assert their own perspectives, and disengage from interactions that are unproductive or emotionally draining. By focusing on self-care and prioritizing emotional well-being, individuals can mitigate the negative impact of judgmental behavior on their mental health and self-esteem.

Furthermore, it is important to adopt a compassionate and empathetic stance when interacting with judgmental people. Rather than viewing them as adversaries or seeking to change their behavior, individuals can approach them with curiosity and understanding. By listening actively and empathetically to their perspectives, individuals can foster open communication and create opportunities for mutual understanding and growth. Additionally, offering validation and support to judgmental people can help alleviate their insecurities and reduce the need for judgment as a coping mechanism.

In some cases, addressing judgmental behavior directly may be necessary for promoting positive change and fostering healthier relationships. When confronted with judgmental comments or behaviors, individuals can assertively communicate their boundaries and express how the judgmental behavior impacts them. Using "I" statements and focusing on specific behaviors rather than attacking the person's character can facilitate constructive dialogue and promote accountability. However, it is essential to approach these conversations with empathy and sensitivity, recognizing that change may take time and require ongoing support and encouragement.

Lastly, cultivating empathy and compassion towards oneself and others is key to navigating judgmental interactions effectively. By practicing self-compassion and embracing imperfection, individuals can develop resilience and confidence in the face of judgment. Similarly, extending compassion towards judgmental people can help break down barriers and foster genuine connections based on mutual respect and understanding. Ultimately, by adopting a mindset of empathy, self-awareness, and assertiveness, individuals can navigate judgmental interactions with grace and resilience, while promoting compassion and understanding in their relationships and communities.

Identifying Judgemental Behaviors

Identifying judgmental behaviors is an essential step in understanding the complex dynamics of human interaction and promoting empathy and understanding in social relationships. In the realm of psychology, recognizing these behaviors involves understanding the underlying thoughts, emotions, and actions that contribute to judgments towards oneself and others.

One common form of judgmental behavior is making negative assumptions or stereotypes about individuals based on superficial characteristics such as appearance, ethnicity, or socioeconomic status. This type of judgment often arises from cognitive biases and societal conditioning, leading individuals to categorize others into simplistic and often inaccurate labels. For example, assuming that someone is lazy or unintelligent based on their clothing or accent reflects a judgmental mindset rooted in prejudice and discrimination.

Another telltale sign of judgmental behavior is the tendency to engage in gossip or spreading rumors about others. When individuals participate in gossip, they often make unfounded assumptions or pass judgment on others' actions or motives without considering the full context of the situation. Gossiping not only perpetuates negative stereotypes and harms relationships but also reflects underlying insecurities and the need for validation through putting others down.

Furthermore, engaging in comparisons and criticisms of others' achievements or lifestyles is indicative of judgmental behavior. Whether it's criticizing someone's career choices, parenting style, or relationship status, making unsolicited judgments about others' life decisions reflects a lack of empathy and respect for individual autonomy. Such behavior often stems from a desire to feel superior or validated in one's own choices, rather than genuinely understanding and appreciating the diversity of human experiences.

Moreover, displaying a lack of empathy or sensitivity towards others' feelings and experiences is a common manifestation of judgmental behavior. This can include invalidating others' emotions, minimizing their struggles, or dismissing their perspectives without genuine consideration. For instance, telling someone to "just get over it" or "stop being so sensitive" reflects a judgmental attitude that fails to recognize the complexity of human emotions and the impact of individual experiences.

Additionally, engaging in passive-aggressive behavior or backhanded compliments can be indicative of underlying judgmental attitudes. Instead of expressing genuine praise or concern, individuals may use subtle or indirect means to convey disapproval or criticism towards others. This form of behavior often reflects underlying resentment or envy, leading individuals to mask their judgmental attitudes behind a facade of politeness or false concern.

Overall, identifying judgmental behaviors requires a keen awareness of one's thoughts, emotions, and actions in social interactions. By recognizing the signs of judgmental behavior, individuals can begin to challenge their own biases and cultivate empathy and understanding towards others. This process involves actively practicing self-reflection, empathy, and open-mindedness, while also being mindful of the impact of one's words and actions on others. Through self-awareness and introspection, individuals can work towards fostering more positive and compassionate relationships, free from the harmful effects of judgmental attitudes and behaviors.

Coping Strategies for Dealing with Judgemental People

Dealing with judgmental people can be challenging, but there are several coping strategies that individuals can employ to navigate such situations effectively. These strategies involve understanding the root causes of judgmental behavior, setting boundaries, practicing empathy, and maintaining self-confidence.

One coping strategy is to recognize that judgmental behavior often stems from the insecurities and biases of the judgmental individual rather than any inherent flaws in oneself. By understanding that judgmental people may project their own insecurities onto others, individuals can avoid taking their judgments personally and instead focus on maintaining their self-esteem and confidence.

Setting boundaries is another crucial coping strategy for dealing with judgmental people. This involves establishing clear limits on what behavior is acceptable and communicating these boundaries assertively but respectfully. For example, if someone makes derogatory comments about your appearance or lifestyle, calmly but firmly assert that such remarks are hurtful and unacceptable. Setting boundaries can help protect one's emotional well-being and prevent further instances of judgmental behavior.

Practicing empathy towards judgmental individuals can also be an effective coping strategy. While it may be challenging to empathize with someone who is critical or dismissive, understanding the underlying reasons for their behavior can help diffuse tension and foster more constructive communication. Recognizing that judgmental people may be struggling with their own insecurities or past traumas can create a sense of compassion and reduce the likelihood of conflict.

Maintaining self-confidence is essential when dealing with judgmental people. By cultivating a strong sense of self-worth and self-assurance, individuals can brush off negative judgments more easily and remain resilient in the face of criticism. Engaging in activities that boost self-esteem, such as practicing self-care, pursuing hobbies, or seeking support from loved ones, can help bolster confidence and reduce the impact of judgmental behavior.

Another coping strategy is to practice assertive communication when confronted with judgmental comments or behavior. Instead of becoming defensive or lashing out, calmly express how the judgmental behavior makes you feel and assert your right to be treated with respect. For example, saying something like, "I understand that you have your opinions, but I would appreciate it if you could refrain from making negative comments about my choices," can help assert boundaries while maintaining a respectful tone.

Additionally, it can be helpful to reframe negative judgments as opportunities for personal growth and learning. Rather than internalizing criticism or allowing it to erode self-esteem, view it as constructive feedback that can help identify areas for improvement or self-reflection. By reframing judgmental comments in a positive light, individuals can turn adversity into an opportunity for self-development and resilience.

In conclusion, coping with judgmental people requires a combination of understanding, assertiveness, empathy, and self-confidence. By recognizing the root causes of judgmental behavior, setting boundaries, practicing empathy, maintaining self-confidence, and reframing negative judgments, individuals can navigate such situations with resilience and grace. Ultimately, coping with judgmental people involves prioritizing one's emotional well-being and remaining true to oneself despite external criticism.

Managing Personal Bias

Managing personal bias is a multifaceted process that involves self-awareness, critical thinking, and a willingness to challenge one's own assumptions and beliefs. Personal biases, whether conscious or unconscious, can influence our perceptions, attitudes, and behavior, often leading to unfair judgments and discriminatory actions towards others. By understanding the psychology behind biases and implementing strategies to mitigate their impact, individuals can strive towards greater fairness, empathy, and inclusivity in their interactions with others.

One key aspect of managing personal bias is developing self-awareness. This involves recognizing and acknowledging our own biases, prejudices, and stereotypes. Many biases operate at a subconscious level, making them difficult to identify without intentional introspection. Engaging in self-reflection and examining our thoughts, feelings, and reactions can help uncover underlying biases and patterns of discriminatory thinking. Techniques such as journaling, meditation, and seeking feedback from others can aid in this process of self-discovery.

Once personal biases have been identified, the next step is to challenge and confront them. This requires cultivating a mindset of critical thinking and openness to new perspectives. Rather than accepting our biases as immutable truths, we must actively question and examine the validity of our assumptions. This may involve seeking out information that contradicts our preconceived notions, engaging in dialogue with individuals from diverse backgrounds, and considering alternative interpretations of situations. By challenging our biases, we can begin to broaden our understanding and empathy towards others.

Another effective strategy for managing personal bias is practicing empathy and perspective-taking. Empathy involves putting oneself in the shoes of others and understanding their thoughts, feelings, and experiences. By empathizing with individuals who are different from ourselves, we can gain insight into their perspectives and develop greater compassion and tolerance. Techniques such as active listening, asking open-ended questions, and seeking to understand rather than judge can facilitate empathetic interactions and help overcome biases based on stereotypes or prejudice.

Cognitive strategies such as cognitive reappraisal and cognitive restructuring can also be useful in managing personal bias. Cognitive reappraisal involves reframing negative or biased thoughts into more balanced and rational ones. For example, if we find ourselves making sweeping generalizations about a certain group of people, we can challenge these stereotypes by considering individual differences and recognizing the inherent complexity of human behavior. Similarly, cognitive restructuring involves actively changing the underlying beliefs and attitudes that fuel biased thinking. This may involve examining the evidence for our beliefs, challenging distorted thinking patterns, and replacing negative or discriminatory beliefs with more positive and inclusive ones.

In addition to individual efforts, creating an environment that promotes diversity, equity, and inclusion is essential for managing personal bias on a societal level. This can include implementing policies and practices that mitigate the impact of bias in areas such as hiring, education, and healthcare, as well as fostering a culture of respect and understanding within communities and organizations. By addressing systemic inequalities and promoting greater awareness and understanding of personal biases, we can work towards a more just and inclusive society for all.

Unconscious Biases and Their Effect on Judgements

Unconscious biases are deeply ingrained beliefs, attitudes, and stereotypes that influence our perceptions, decisions, and behaviors without our conscious awareness. These biases operate automatically and can impact various aspects of our lives, including how we judge others. Despite our best intentions, unconscious biases can lead to unfair or discriminatory judgments, often perpetuating inequalities and prejudices in society.

One common type of unconscious bias is implicit bias, which refers to the attitudes and stereotypes that affect our understanding, actions, and decisions in an unconscious manner. Implicit biases can manifest in various forms, such as racial bias, gender bias, age bias, and socio-economic bias, among others. These biases are often formed through socialization, cultural norms, and media representations, and can shape our perceptions of different social groups.

For example, research has shown that people tend to associate certain characteristics or traits with specific social groups, leading to biased judgments and behaviors. These biases can influence how we perceive and interact with others, affecting decisions in areas such as hiring, promotion, education, and criminal justice.

One of the key effects of unconscious biases on judgments is the perpetuation of stereotypes and prejudices. When individuals rely on unconscious biases to make judgments about others, they may inadvertently reinforce existing stereotypes and discrimination. For example, if a hiring manager has unconscious biases against certain racial or ethnic groups, they may be more likely to overlook qualified candidates from those groups, leading to disparities in employment opportunities.

Unconscious biases can also impact interpersonal interactions and relationships. When individuals hold unconscious biases against others, they may treat them differently based on stereotypes or preconceived notions, leading to strained relationships and misunderstandings. For example, if someone holds unconscious biases against individuals of a certain gender, they may be less likely to listen to their ideas or value their contributions in a professional setting.

Furthermore, unconscious biases can affect decision-making processes, leading to biased outcomes that perpetuate inequalities. Research has shown that even well-intentioned individuals can be influenced by unconscious biases when making decisions, such as evaluating job candidates, assessing student performance, or determining guilt or innocence in legal proceedings. These biases can result in unfair treatment and disparities in outcomes for marginalized groups.

Addressing unconscious biases requires a combination of awareness, education, and proactive measures. Individuals can start by examining their own biases and challenging stereotypical thinking patterns through self-reflection and education. Engaging in conversations about unconscious bias and diversity training can also help raise awareness and promote understanding of the impact of biases on judgments and behaviors.

In addition to individual efforts, organizations and institutions can implement policies and practices to mitigate the influence of unconscious biases in decision-making processes. This can include implementing blind recruitment processes, where identifying information such as name, gender, and race is removed from job applications to reduce the impact of biases. Diversity training programs and workshops can also help employees recognize and address unconscious biases in the workplace.

Overall, understanding the impact of unconscious biases on judgments is essential for promoting fairness, equity, and inclusivity in society. By raising awareness of these biases and taking proactive steps to address them, individuals and organizations can work towards creating a more just and equitable world for all.

Techniques for Overcoming Personal Bias

Overcoming personal bias is a complex and challenging process that requires self-awareness, introspection, and a willingness to challenge deeply ingrained beliefs and attitudes. While biases are a natural part of human cognition, they can lead to unfair judgments and discriminatory behavior if left unchecked. Fortunately, there are several techniques and strategies that individuals can employ to overcome personal bias and cultivate a more open-minded and inclusive mindset.

One effective technique for overcoming personal bias is education and exposure to diverse perspectives. By actively seeking out information and experiences that challenge existing beliefs and assumptions, individuals can broaden their understanding of different cultures, backgrounds, and viewpoints. This can involve reading books, articles, and studies on topics related to diversity and inclusion, attending workshops or seminars, and engaging in conversations with people from diverse backgrounds. Exposure to diverse perspectives can help individuals recognize and challenge their own biases, leading to greater empathy and understanding.

Another technique for overcoming personal bias is mindfulness and self-reflection. Mindfulness practices, such as meditation and deep breathing exercises, can help individuals become more aware of their thoughts, emotions, and reactions. By observing their own thought patterns and emotional responses without judgment, individuals can begin to identify and challenge automatic biases and stereotypes. Self-reflection involves critically examining one's own beliefs and attitudes, considering where they come from and how they influence perceptions and behaviors. This process of introspection can help individuals recognize and address biases that may be operating at a subconscious level.

Additionally, practicing empathy and perspective-taking can help individuals overcome personal bias. Empathy involves the ability to understand and share the feelings of others, while perspective-taking involves putting oneself in someone else's shoes and seeing the world from their point of view. By actively listening to others, seeking to understand their experiences and perspectives, and empathizing with their feelings, individuals can develop greater compassion and empathy towards others, reducing the influence of personal bias on judgments and behavior.

Another effective technique for overcoming personal bias is cognitive restructuring, which involves challenging and reframing negative or stereotypical thoughts. When individuals catch themselves making biased judgments or assumptions, they can consciously challenge those thoughts by considering alternative explanations and perspectives. This can involve asking questions such as "What evidence do I have to support this belief?" or "Is there a more charitable interpretation of this person's behavior?" By actively challenging and reframing biased thoughts, individuals can gradually rewire their brain to think more inclusively and empathetically.

Finally, seeking feedback from others can be a valuable tool for overcoming personal bias. Trusted friends, family members, or colleagues can provide valuable insights and perspectives on one's attitudes and behaviors, helping to identify blind spots and areas for improvement. By soliciting feedback and being open to constructive criticism, individuals can gain valuable insights into their own biases and take steps to address them.

In conclusion, overcoming personal bias is a challenging but essential endeavor for promoting fairness, equity, and inclusivity in society. By employing techniques such as education, mindfulness, empathy, cognitive restructuring, and seeking feedback, individuals can cultivate a more open-minded and inclusive mindset, leading to more positive interactions and relationships with others.

Psychology of Decision Making and Judgement

Decision-making and judgment are fundamental aspects of human cognition, influencing how individuals perceive, evaluate, and respond to the world around them. While decision-making involves choosing between different options or courses of action, judgment involves forming opinions or evaluations about people, events, or situations. The psychology of decision-making and judgment encompasses a wide range of cognitive processes, biases, and heuristics that shape how individuals make choices and form judgments.

One key aspect of the psychology of decision-making and judgment is the concept of heuristics, or mental shortcuts, that individuals use to simplify complex decision-making tasks. Heuristics allow individuals to make decisions quickly and efficiently, but they can also lead to errors and biases in judgment. For example, the availability heuristic involves judging the likelihood of an event based on how easily it comes to mind. This can lead individuals to overestimate the likelihood of rare or memorable events and underestimate the likelihood of common events.

Another important concept in the psychology of decision-making and judgment is the influence of emotions on decision-making processes. Research has shown that emotions play a significant role in shaping how individuals make decisions and form judgments. For example, individuals may be more risk-averse when experiencing fear or anxiety, leading them to avoid taking chances or making bold decisions. Similarly, individuals may be more likely to rely on stereotypes or prejudices when experiencing negative emotions such as anger or frustration.

Cognitive biases also play a significant role in the psychology of decision-making and judgment. These biases are systematic errors in thinking that can lead individuals to make irrational or illogical decisions. One common cognitive bias is confirmation bias, which involves seeking out information that confirms pre-existing beliefs or hypotheses while ignoring or discounting contradictory evidence. Confirmation bias can lead individuals to make decisions based on incomplete or biased information, resulting in flawed judgments.

Another cognitive bias that influences decision-making and judgment is anchoring bias, which involves relying too heavily on initial information or "anchors" when making decisions. For example, individuals may be influenced by the first piece of information they encounter when making a decision, even if it is irrelevant or misleading. This can lead to errors in judgment and decision-making, as individuals may fail to consider all relevant information or alternatives.

Social factors also play a significant role in the psychology of decision-making and judgment. Research has shown that individuals are often influenced by the opinions and behaviors of others when making decisions or forming judgments. This phenomenon, known as social influence, can manifest in various ways, including conformity to group norms, peer pressure, and the influence of authority figures. Social influence can lead individuals to make decisions that they would not make independently or to form judgments based on social expectations rather than objective evidence.

In conclusion, the psychology of decision-making and judgment is a complex and multifaceted field that encompasses a wide range of cognitive processes, biases, and social influences. Understanding these factors is essential for gaining insight into how individuals make decisions and form judgments, as well as for identifying strategies to mitigate the effects of biases and improve decision-making outcomes. By examining the underlying mechanisms of decision-making and judgment, researchers can develop interventions and strategies to help individuals make more informed and rational choices, leading to better outcomes in various domains of life.

The Relationship Between Decision Making and Judgement

Decision-making and judgment are intricately connected processes that play a vital role in human cognition and behavior. While decision-making involves choosing between alternative courses of action, judgment involves forming opinions or evaluations about people, events, or situations. Understanding the relationship between decision-making and judgment is essential for comprehending how individuals perceive, evaluate, and respond to the world around them.

One way to understand the relationship between decision-making and judgment is to examine the cognitive processes involved in both. Decision-making typically involves several stages, including identifying and defining the problem, generating alternative solutions, evaluating the alternatives, making a choice, and implementing and evaluating the decision. Throughout this process, individuals rely on various cognitive mechanisms, such as heuristics, emotions, and biases, to simplify complex decision-making tasks and reach a conclusion.

Judgment, on the other hand, is the process of forming opinions or evaluations about people, events, or situations based on available information. While decision-making involves choosing between alternatives, judgment involves assessing the qualities or characteristics of a particular option or entity. Individuals often rely on cognitive processes similar to those involved in decision-making, such as heuristics, emotions, and biases, when forming judgments.

One key aspect of the relationship between decision-making and judgment is the influence of cognitive biases. Cognitive biases are systematic errors in thinking that can distort decision-making and judgment processes. For example, confirmation bias, which involves seeking out information that confirms pre-existing beliefs or hypotheses while ignoring contradictory evidence, can affect both decision-making and judgment. Individuals may selectively attend to information that supports their chosen course of action or reinforces their existing beliefs, leading to biased decisions and judgments.

Another important factor in the relationship between decision-making and judgment is the role of emotions. Emotions can influence both decision-making and judgment processes by shaping individuals' preferences, priorities, and evaluations. For example, individuals may be more risk-averse when experiencing fear or anxiety, leading them to avoid taking chances or making bold decisions. Similarly, individuals may form more negative judgments about others when experiencing negative emotions such as anger or frustration.

Social factors also play a significant role in shaping both decision-making and judgment processes. Individuals are often influenced by the opinions and behaviors of others when making decisions or forming judgments. Social influence can manifest in various ways, including conformity to group norms, peer pressure, and the influence of authority figures. Social factors can affect decision-making and judgment by shaping individuals' perceptions of what is socially acceptable or desirable, leading them to make decisions or form judgments that align with social expectations.

In conclusion, decision-making and judgment are closely related processes that play a crucial role in human cognition and behavior. Both involve complex cognitive processes, such as heuristics, emotions, and biases, that can influence individuals' choices and evaluations. By understanding the relationship between decision-making and judgment, researchers can gain insight into how individuals perceive, evaluate, and respond to the world around them, leading to a deeper understanding of human behavior and cognition.

Cognitive Mechanisms Involved in Decision Making

Decision-making is a complex cognitive process that involves various mechanisms aimed at selecting the best course of action among several alternatives. Understanding the cognitive mechanisms involved in decision-making is crucial for comprehending how individuals make choices and judgments in different contexts.

One fundamental cognitive mechanism involved in decision-making is the use of heuristics. Heuristics are mental shortcuts or rules of thumb that individuals employ to simplify decision-making tasks and arrive at judgments quickly. One commonly observed heuristic is the availability heuristic, where individuals base their judgments on the ease with which relevant examples come to mind. For instance, individuals may perceive a particular event as more common or likely if they can readily recall similar instances from memory.

Another important cognitive mechanism in decision-making is the use of affective responses or emotions. Emotions can play a significant role in guiding decision-making by influencing individuals' preferences, priorities, and evaluations. For example, individuals may be more likely to choose options that elicit positive emotions, such as happiness or excitement, while avoiding options associated with negative emotions, such as fear or sadness. Additionally, emotions can serve as valuable signals or cues that help individuals evaluate the potential outcomes of their decisions.

Furthermore, cognitive biases are pervasive cognitive mechanisms that can impact decision-making processes. Cognitive biases are systematic errors in thinking that can distort individuals' perceptions and lead to irrational or suboptimal decision-making outcomes. For instance, confirmation bias is a cognitive bias where individuals tend to seek out information that confirms their existing beliefs or hypotheses while ignoring contradictory evidence. Confirmation bias can influence decision-making by causing individuals to selectively attend to information that supports their preferred course of action while disregarding evidence that suggests alternative options.

Moreover, individuals often rely on mental representations or schemas to organize and interpret information during decision-making. Schemas are cognitive structures that represent knowledge about specific concepts, events, or situations. These mental representations help individuals make sense of the world around them by providing a framework for understanding and interpreting new information. For example, individuals may use schemas about different types of products or services to guide their decision-making when comparing options or making purchasing decisions.

Additionally, decision-making can be influenced by the interplay between automatic and controlled cognitive processes. Automatic processes are fast, effortless, and involuntary responses to stimuli, while controlled processes are slower, deliberate, and conscious responses that require cognitive effort. In many decision-making situations, individuals may rely on automatic processes, such as intuition or gut feelings, to make quick judgments or choices. However, in more complex or uncertain situations, individuals may engage in controlled processes, such as careful deliberation or systematic analysis, to make decisions.

Furthermore, decision-making is often influenced by contextual factors, such as social norms, cultural values, and situational cues. Individuals' decisions and judgments may vary depending on the social context in which they occur, as well as the cultural norms and expectations that shape individuals' behavior. For example, individuals may conform to group norms or adhere to cultural conventions when making decisions in social settings, leading to decisions that align with societal expectations.

In conclusion, decision-making is a multifaceted cognitive process that involves various mechanisms, including heuristics, emotions, cognitive biases, schemas, and the interplay between automatic and controlled processes. By understanding these cognitive mechanisms, researchers can gain insight into how individuals make choices and judgments in different contexts, leading to a deeper understanding of human behavior and cognition.

Perception and Judgement

Perception and judgment are intertwined processes that significantly influence how individuals interpret, evaluate, and respond to the world around them. Understanding the relationship between perception and judgment is essential for comprehending how individuals form opinions, make decisions, and interact with others in various contexts.

Perception refers to the way individuals interpret and make sense of sensory information from their environment. It involves the brain's processing of sensory inputs, such as sight, sound, touch, taste, and smell, to create a meaningful understanding of the world. Perception is influenced by various factors, including past experiences, cultural background, expectations, and context. For example, two individuals may perceive the same object or event differently based on their unique perceptual filters and interpretations.

Judgment, on the other hand, involves the process of evaluating and forming opinions or conclusions about people, events, objects, or situations based on perceived information. Judgments can be influenced by cognitive biases, emotions, social norms, personal beliefs, and values. Individuals often make judgments automatically and unconsciously, drawing on their perceptions to assess and categorize stimuli in their environment. However, judgments can also be influenced by deliberate reasoning and conscious reflection.

The relationship between perception and judgment is complex and reciprocal. Perception serves as the foundation upon which judgments are built, as individuals rely on their sensory experiences and interpretations to form opinions and make decisions. At the same time, judgments can also shape perception by influencing individuals' attention, interpretation, and memory of sensory information. For example, individuals may selectively attend to information that aligns with their existing judgments while ignoring or discounting contradictory evidence.

Cognitive psychologists have identified several cognitive mechanisms that underlie the relationship between perception and judgment. One such mechanism is the use of mental shortcuts or heuristics to simplify decision-making tasks. These heuristics, such as availability heuristic and representativeness heuristic, can influence individuals' judgments by biasing their perceptions and leading to systematic errors in reasoning.

Emotions also play a crucial role in the relationship between perception and judgment. Emotional responses can color individuals' perceptions of stimuli and influence the judgments they form. For example, individuals may perceive ambiguous situations more negatively when they are in a state of fear or anxiety, leading to more critical or harsh judgments.

Furthermore, social factors, such as cultural norms and societal expectations, can shape both perception and judgment. Cultural differences in perception can lead to variations in judgment across different cultural groups. For instance, research has shown that individuals from collectivist cultures may prioritize group harmony and interdependence in their judgments, whereas individuals from individualistic cultures may prioritize personal autonomy and independence.

In conclusion, perception and judgment are intertwined processes that significantly impact how individuals understand, evaluate, and respond to the world around them. Perception serves as the foundation upon which judgments are built, while judgments, in turn, can influence perception. Understanding the relationship between perception and judgment is essential for gaining insight into human cognition and behavior and addressing issues related to bias, stereotyping, and prejudice.

How Perception Influences Judgement

Perception plays a crucial role in shaping the way individuals form judgments about the world around them. It serves as the lens through which people interpret and make sense of sensory information, ultimately influencing the decisions they make and the opinions they form. Understanding how perception influences judgment is essential for gaining insight into human behavior and addressing biases and prejudices that may arise in various contexts.

One way perception influences judgment is through the process of selective attention. Selective attention refers to individuals' tendency to focus on certain aspects of their environment while ignoring others. This selective focus can be influenced by factors such as personal interests, past experiences, and current goals. For example, if someone has a negative perception of a particular group of people, they may selectively attend to information that confirms their preconceived beliefs while disregarding evidence that contradicts them. This selective attention can lead to biased judgments and reinforce existing stereotypes and prejudices.

Another way perception influences judgment is through the process of interpretation. Once sensory information is perceived, individuals must interpret it to derive meaning and understanding. However, interpretation is subjective and can be influenced by factors such as cultural background, beliefs, and expectations. For instance, two people may interpret the same ambiguous behavior differently based on their unique perceptual filters and past experiences. These interpretations can shape the judgments individuals form about others and the world around them.

Perception also influences judgment through the process of memory. Once sensory information is perceived and interpreted, it is stored in memory for future reference. However, memory is not always accurate and can be influenced by various factors, including biases and emotions. Individuals may remember information that is consistent with their existing beliefs and judgments more readily than information that contradicts them. This selective memory can reinforce existing biases and prejudices and influence future judgments and decision-making processes.

Furthermore, perception influences judgment through the process of categorization and stereotyping. Categorization involves grouping stimuli into categories based on shared characteristics, while stereotyping involves attributing certain traits or characteristics to members of a particular group. These categorizations and stereotypes can influence the judgments individuals form about others, often leading to unfair and biased assessments.

For example, if someone perceives members of a certain ethnic group as aggressive, they may stereotype all members of that group as being aggressive, regardless of individual differences.

Additionally, perception can influence judgment through the process of emotional arousal. Emotional arousal can affect individuals' perceptions of stimuli and influence the judgments they form. For example, if someone is in a state of fear or anger, they may perceive ambiguous situations more negatively and make harsher judgments as a result. Conversely, positive emotions such as happiness and empathy can lead to more positive perceptions and judgments.

In conclusion, perception plays a critical role in shaping the judgments individuals form about the world around them. It influences judgment through processes such as selective attention, interpretation, memory, categorization, and emotional arousal. Understanding how perception influences judgment is essential for addressing biases and prejudices and promoting fair and objective decision-making in various contexts.

Changing Perceptions to Improve Judgement.

Changing perceptions to improve judgment is a complex yet essential aspect of personal growth and societal progress. Perception, the process through which individuals interpret and make sense of sensory information, directly influences the judgments they form about themselves, others, and the world around them. However, perceptions are not fixed; they can be influenced and modified through various means, ultimately leading to more accurate and informed judgments.

One effective way to change perceptions and improve judgment is through education and exposure to diverse perspectives. By learning about different cultures, beliefs, and experiences, individuals can broaden their understanding of the world and develop empathy and compassion towards others. Exposure to diverse perspectives can challenge existing biases and stereotypes, leading to more open-minded and nuanced judgments. For example, educational programs that promote cultural awareness and diversity can help individuals recognize the richness and complexity of human experiences, thereby reducing prejudice and discrimination.

Another strategy for changing perceptions and improving judgment is through cognitive restructuring. Cognitive restructuring involves identifying and challenging irrational or distorted thoughts and beliefs that contribute to negative judgments. By examining the evidence for and against their beliefs, individuals can develop more rational and balanced perspectives. This process can help individuals recognize and correct cognitive biases, such as confirmation bias and stereotyping, leading to more accurate and fair-minded judgments. Cognitive-behavioral therapy (CBT) is a widely used therapeutic approach that employs cognitive restructuring techniques to help individuals overcome negative thought patterns and improve judgment.

Furthermore, fostering empathy and perspective-taking can facilitate changes in perception and judgment. Empathy, the ability to understand and share the feelings of others, allows individuals to see the world from different vantage points and appreciate the diversity of human experiences. By actively engaging in perspective-taking exercises, such as imagining oneself in someone else's shoes or considering alternative viewpoints, individuals can develop greater empathy and compassion towards others. This enhanced empathy can lead to more empathetic and understanding judgments, as individuals are better able to appreciate the complexities of human behavior and motivation.

Moreover, promoting critical thinking skills can aid in changing perceptions and improving judgment. Critical thinking involves analyzing information objectively, evaluating arguments and evidence, and making informed decisions. By teaching individuals how to critically evaluate information and question their own assumptions and biases, critical thinking can help individuals develop more reasoned and evidence-based judgments. Education programs that emphasize critical thinking skills, such as logic and reasoning courses, can empower individuals to approach issues with greater skepticism and discernment, ultimately leading to more informed and rational judgments.

In addition, fostering self-awareness and mindfulness can facilitate changes in perception and judgment. Self-awareness involves being conscious of one's thoughts, feelings, and behaviors, while mindfulness involves being present and attentive to the present moment without judgment. By practicing self-reflection and mindfulness techniques, individuals can become more aware of their own biases and automatic judgments, allowing them to pause and reconsider their assumptions before making decisions. This increased self-awareness can lead to more deliberate and conscious judgments, as individuals become attuned to their own cognitive processes and biases.

In conclusion, changing perceptions to improve judgment is a multifaceted process that involves education, cognitive restructuring, empathy, critical thinking, and self-awareness. By actively challenging biases and stereotypes, fostering empathy and perspective-taking, promoting critical thinking skills, and cultivating self-awareness and mindfulness, individuals can develop more accurate, fair-minded, and empathetic judgments. These efforts are essential for promoting social harmony, fostering mutual understanding, and building a more just and equitable society.

Have Questions / Comments?

This book was designed to cover as much as possible but I know I have probably missed something, or some new amazing discovery that has just come out.

If you notice something missing or have a question that I failed to answer, please get in touch and let me know. If I can, I will email you an answer and also update the book so others can also benefit from it.

Thanks For Being Awesome :)

Submit Your Questions / Comments At:

https://xspurts.com/posts/questions

Get Another Book Free

We love writing and have produced a huge number of books.

For being one of our amazing readers, we would love to offer you another book we have created, 100% free.

To claim this limited time special offer, simply go to the site below and enter your name and email address.

You will then receive one of my great books, direct to your email account, 100% free!

https://xspurts.com/posts/free-book-offer